Praise for *Lyre*

'Drawing on the deepest resources of antipodean poetics, *Lyre* hymns the created world in all its prodigious diversity. It is funny, reverent, full of curious facts, and crazily ambitious. A triumph.'

J. M. COETZEE

'Stuart Cooke invites us to a fabulous, exciting, wonderful experiment: what does it take to make oneself capable of feeling the poetry of every form of existence? What does it take to decode the poetry of experimenting, experiencing life? Cooke actually writes *toward* beings, and not about them or on them, seeking how to convey in *our* writing the way each organic and inorganic being writes (of) its own existence. Cosmopolitical poetry, or geopoetry: his poetry transforms what is seen into what is heard (melodic pixels: cries, crunching sand, murmurs, calls, crashing waves), what is heard into what is tasted (flavours of oceans, marshes, clouds, bodies, fruits), what is tasted into what is smelled (scents of seabed salt from sweet oxygen), what is smelled into what is felt, and what is felt into movement (dances of enduring life, momentum, convergence and friction, connections, desires and importances, compositions, migrations, territories, respirations, inspirations, aspirations…), movement into writing (geopoetry), writing into drawing (graphopoetry: gulf estuaries, waves, rocks, flickering lights of fireflies, optical epics on the pages), and, finally, drawing into enacted stories, as nourished by knowledge as they are undisciplined.'

VINCIANE DESPRET

'These vibrational songs of selection listen in to the metabolic essays of life forms, imbricated in human exchange, across a wide swath of the southern hemisphere. Cooke's *Lyre* sounds the depths of alien intelligence, in the nearby abyss between disciplines, languages, bodies, and in the drift of new yet barely discerned continents. Shaped poetry was never so planetary, nor as porous to other ways of seeing and knowing – an astonishing act of attention.'

JONATHAN SKINNER

Stuart Cooke

Stuart was born in 1980 and grew up in Sydney and Hobart. He has travelled widely and lived in various parts of Latin America, the Philippines, the United Kingdom and the United States. He now lives in Brisbane, on Jagera and Turrbal country, where he lectures in creative writing and literary studies at Griffith University. Widely published as a poet, critic and translator, *Lyre* is his third collection of poems.

Other books by the author

Poetry

Opera (2016)
Edge Music (2011)

Translation

The Blackbird by Gianni Siccardi (2018)
George Dyuŋgayan's Bulu Line: A West Kimberley Song Cycle (2014)

Criticism

Speaking the Earth's Languages: A Theory for Australian-Chilean Postcolonial Poetics (2013)

Lyre

STUART COOKE

UWA PUBLISHING

First published in 2019 by
UWA Publishing
Crawley, Western Australia 6009
www.uwap.uwa.edu.au

UWAP is an imprint of UWA Publishing,
a division of The University of Western Australia.

THE UNIVERSITY OF WESTERN AUSTRALIA

ISBN: 978-1-76080-034-5

A catalogue record for this book is available from the National Library of Australia

Cover design by Ten Deer Sigh
Cover image of lyrebird by Hein Nouwens and background by Mariya Emchenko, both from Shutterstock
Typeset in Minion by Lasertype
Printed by McPherson's Printing Group

This project has been assisted by the Australian Government through the Australia Council, its arts funding and advisory body.

Australian Government | Australia Council for the Arts

uwapublishing

MIX
Paper from responsible sources
FSC® C001695

For Gina,
with apologies for all the charismatic megafauna.

One writes always for animals...
This does not mean writing about
one's dog, one's cat...It does not
mean making animals speak. It
means writing as a rat draws a line or
flicks its tail, as a bird casts a sound,
as a feline slinks or sinks in sleep.

Gilles Deleuze

Contents

Nephology 1

— sea

Oceanic Manta Ray 7
Whaleshark 19
Pacific Green Turtle 25
Western Clownfish 31

— inter

Shallow Estuary 37
Mangroves 41
Sand-bubbler Crab 51
Fireflies 59
Gecko 65
Magpie 75
Stray Cat 81

— hinter

Eastern Whipbird 93
Pinatubo Volcano 100
Tarsier 119
Satin Bowerbird 125
Moth Orchid 131
King Parrot 137
Red-necked Pademelon 153
Antarctic Beech 161
Albert's Lyrebird 169
Fallen Myrtle Trunk 181

—land

Housefly 187
Tea Tree 195
Spinifex Termite Mound 201
Hamersley 221
Lake Mungo 227

Notes 257
Acknowledgements 261

Nephology

a: hint

orographic ferment
over mountains on my body
there are eight heads
a pool of air a fork
of cracked cerulean lightning
jagging
down the sky's physics

nephology or cloud
physics warm frost
ekes quanta earth's
slow bleed song
of morning in a barnacle
an invisible star's distilled angst

rising
sing to bloom
salty mineral mass
dusty momentum
hygroscopic and spiralling sea

into sand into shell
that chilled
sink sucks heat
into burnt white branches

milky crystal algal
infestation
the absence of condensation
a nuclei's quick scent

eucalyptus rising like
vapour
convective lifting solar

erupting into matter
a starlit

gravity

cooled

to dewpoint

to the seeds

of

b: evolve

densely packed sunlight
its characteristic white
its whole tenor soaked
by soil unfolding
into thought

spoken slowly
cooked children of seed
hesitant buds
of spun cast flossed
coin

scatters labels words
curved to tense
in a gust's labile edge
grammar's darkening
in the near-infrared

bushfire blonde
wild as rime thinks
with that huge stock of porous
mode a stone
turning threshold solar

gas acts
of silence are disappearance
[0] pretence a back-
ground's bleached code
troubles speechlessness

feeble cups of
radioactive method
pressed against
the ear rumbling
like a mammoth's bone

twine of thinnest
snakes clasps at deed
        scrawls mature
thunderheads blood-
red colossus through a parent's

prolific noise
the wind's bluish proliferation
scatters of cumuli
        parables leaning on
fallen trunks filled

with cosmos marrow
a mossy tinge of
ice to cohere
along the canopy
        or descend into fume

        droplets of rays
absorbed on a seared sheet
rippling with
cumulonimbus green
is an imminent sign

c: burst

ratiformis lenticularis and castellanus stratiformis species in sheets of

dry amnesia anamnesis aches in the cloudy iris that

cold brawl do youm crawl gelid belly cranium

of snow sodden lumber gone to haze

on cumuliform's convection palms fr

ayed through lenticularis moun

tain-wave alto-stratus and nimbo-stratus ragged
sheets of stratus fractus ragged cumulus ratty showers

of guerrilla sky flickering along horizon's nerve freely

convective cumulus swathes of scrubby turrets of
castellanus convective patches of cirrus tufted floccus

their uncinus filaments with upturned hooks

with indigo and spissatus mer

ged into dense clumps one except

ion is fibratus with cirrostratus of the s

pecies nebulosus yourm inversion of land and heaven

creates diffusion lacks structure an oaken reliquary a sad sonata shining above a bolt stung by

nyunga singing above it all the public blaze cotton shocked spo

spoke the skin of the earth

Oceanic Manta Ray

yourm thin fossil moves years into midnight belongs / to the mobulidae the largest ray the shape of blood beating & cells dividing of continent & island a mucus / sketch a stingray's tail sin stinplanktivores

zooplankton

copepods

mysid shrimps

arrow worms

ger bottom feeder water / strainer youm draw the vortex with / whalesharks we kill for yourm gills' russet sponge youm rest / in the pelagic make periodic visits / to reefs and seamounts for

a metabolic essay a dark mat rippling / slowly over coral plains the surface grips /
mind swallow and dive the night heaves / slices yourm emergence yourm flexible / fibres
cleaning wander / the globe hugging coasts with island / groups offshore pinnacles growing bigger but /
as if from a dream / youm merge again with the gloomy

youm reply with the weight of the alien planet
to tell youm about my land we keep inhaling this minute atmosphere
for prayer frilling to points to swoop to swoon I want
complexity that territory from which we strayed in our quest
spark of message the crossed threshold of lexical
slicing human from the canvas with spear's indomitable
melody spear eyed by chest dance that whole plane
blabble blurbs chuckle dirge deep pitch poetry humid
undulating ready to close back into slow wave swoop slow
social travelling a node for parasites and remoras a split a black slip
with the weight of yourm great brain patiently mating
by powerful beats bending yourm bowl of truths
an ontology of perpetual motion driven
youm stop youm start to sink through the column
yourm knowing leaves me with shadow if
of contrary response gifted with size wisdom
feel the floor through water's reverb a geology
youm carve gritty field introduce tranquility

the wavering spill of dripping light
like a barnacle youm breach / flight with magical wing muscle / flicked spray, upheaval
glimmering in the raggedy / slew of fantasies their fluid contours leathery / pulse
cut from our tiny skulls slide / swept & glimmer for morsels
capacity of nowhere / greeny and
cleaving

morphed black
to navy-grey
and brown a T-
pattern a black/white divide no
gradient pastel
undersides spot patterned
unique blotch and scar patterns
a dormant spine
waits at the base of the tail

tagged by a storm of slithers
each silver stroke of wake
nibbles yourm merest refuse
floating island/oasis,
parasites blossom in yourm being
in yourm pharynx yourm gills
around yourm mouth slopping in the mucus
on yourm back

yourm itchy umwelt / feeds on yourm
with ectoparasites drags on yourm
with hitchhikers remora suck
into abrasions and sores
the constant burn of remora swarms
around and inside yourm bulk

cleaners set up shop at outcrops and
bommies where yourm beeline
to play in languid circuits
if a bite's too hard
yourm fly into speed
a stream of fleeing cleaners
pouring from yourm body

blue-streaked and lunar
tailed wrasse trail
behind flood
yourm surface plumb
yourm function

two ashen remora
cling upside down
with dorsal fins-cum-suction
cups

golden in the gully
three brazen trevally
bow riding the pressure
of yourm dome like dolphins
piloting yourm voyage
from the shade of yourm shelter

a clarion angelfish cleans ecto-
parasites from yourm tail
off Mexico

appearing to balance on yourm tail youm stand above the

bed the cleaner fish scurry / three slim remoras circle yourm unusual statue

if I called to youm once, les llamé en castellano, manta, manta / that cloak that blanket that blanket-like trap I once used to catch youm

if I see youm from the shore youm're close to shark but flapping lolling / shy as an asymptote a murky blob of paint / a submerged slick heading south with the sweep

Whaleshark

through yourm voice flows great calm the seeds of
minimal matters macroalgae / plankton nektonic life
with yourm mouth open scull / volumes and let them p
sieves modified gill / rakers the filter / pads sluice matter
youm look to space / spearing the crypt before sinking back
swallow comets their ancient vectors the loops of hemispheres
yourm voice leaves / yourm ode returns youm fill / the silty glo-
yourm name glimmers in pale coin code / a capacious mouth a very
front a wide flat / head rounded snout tiny / eyes the spiracle is just
metres & 9 tonnes a grooved ovivaporous giant a filter / feeder *ca ong Sir*
the adult tale becomes semi-lunate / the females are larger / than the males
know us close youm tantalise / with the possibility of touch I / see youm fro-
lungs burst / a dawdler shifting yourm great posterior drifting / at uman speed b-
rent / cool as gift of marine reverie humble / symphonies recall yourm storm docile
are typically / offshore youm live in the deep / return to glide along seafronts when co-
ummers into spring / vortex of one hundred years twisted / into conical feasts still we hu-
t after / feet but youm find depths where the sun bends towards youm / waits for youm bes-
youm stumble towards beginnings migrate / to feed breed call it happiness / everything's surge yourm life
buffeted by brackish algal tang by saline / sweetness solitary generally youm group / seasonally at cer-

thunder and sleet youm feed on
and clouds of sperm ram schools
-ass through the gills / special black
from water occasionally / youm cough
to flush / food though yourm rakers youm
string oceans together with yourm breath when
om the largest fish / the speckled smiling mattress
large moment a distinctively wide mouth at head's very
behind the eye / finely carved soft wood or grey rubber 10
Fish pez dama butanding a pair / each of dorsal & pectoral fins
the skin's an inch thick like a sine wave / any wave youm rise to
m above follow yourm descent / searching yourm beady eye but my
efore youm slide beneath / closing curtains of sediment usually indiffe-
beats of / kelp drive those sad tropical sighs / yourm elaborate warm youm
ral's spawning / in Útila in the Yucatán / in Donsol and Batangas youm filter s-
nt youm and caught in slicks / youm're followed by wee mouths with thrashing fee-
ide the shelf all the poems / huddling underneath youm dream of youm Sir / Shark Sir
is cruise / the lean ones hitch rides the food / flowing straight into yourm gut / in the core of sleep / spir-
tain sites during plankton blooms mass / coral spawnings at Ningaloo motion / is yourm riverine sea-

acles echo their shadows microscopic cries / enter the wash the massive docile / fish that upon reaching
son aqua fowl youm know water / control water youm understand the night / read its infinite answer

what shall be is moonward, infant idlers
    if what is floats up, unbearable
    the great belt of rupture
the face or what it says
    not in the husk that shatters
but in the song that stumbles

the surface translates the abyss:::::
and yet youm accept / the spikey words that wait

peaceful dance of slumber thing
gentle looking through thing
big lumbering happy turning

opening yourm being to the blue
the timid phantoms rest
on yourm lips

Pacific Green Turtle

yourm sure horn trumpets the end

keeps sure radius
little mouth, yourm lunar sight
and unhooked beak, nibbling
yourm petite pate, short snout
graceful swimmer
naked limbs like flippers
a chocolate spot in the middle of limbs
amber-hued, dark, yellow-lined limbs
the greens of the Atlantic, of the East Pacific
the greenish fat beneath the shell
a name is a greenish skin

about above
marbled shells compress anxieties
or marbled variegated rays
shaped tears arrange change into spotted
but names aren't shells, their bronze or olive fig-

yourm drifting bulk
wide carapace wafting
matt-wet, a sleek
yourm opulent home, rainbow-brown
of yourm supreme sign
is a bursting shell
night climbs the dais, each star

yourm equatorial line has sprouted

for a bygone planet's exiles
angel weaves crowns of seaweed
the bow, this liquid plane—a ship-wrecked
tossed prospects—below
Sails suspend

hidden in the mist
and cover them, hundreds of them
youm dig a hole in the darkness
after shallow water sex
night events
tropical beach nests

between feeding and nesting
into yourm everlasting journey
where youm hatch at the precise entry
thousands of miles to spawning grounds
floobin, swim
ohbedoe be, hoodie
niggedly, moody
push off, yourm round skirt
shift off, up
hang in bays and lagoons, gnawing, nibbling
plomp down on coral pasture
youm grow to graze in shallows, lush seagrass meadows
from meat, from pelagic absence

when we build feasts on yourm beaches
in nets, and so many more lives end
then youm're slivered by propellers or drown
and long-legged mammals
jackals, then más, y más, to tiger sharks
foxes and golden
in shorebirds and crabs, red
the end comes in the beginning
Stories fall like glowing worms

sapphire crown uncovered by a wing
of a bird that sleeps in branches
yourm poems are of visions
at rest, sleepy eyes

wavering above it
qualifying certainty
yourm hundreds of kilos oolging
an architecture of haze
where crags become cloudform, youm see

trodden upon by monumental echoes
over fields of sunken sunlight
and youm clap yourm gracile wings
bathes yourm tissues in blood
explode yourm breast, yourm next inspiration
sail over the waves / the troughs
this life submerged, yourm desires

youm will glimpse a century
that 1%
youm die, and die, but youm that remain
the flags of crabs attack, flocks of gulls shatter the pressure
yourm miniature flippers scratching for purchase
Months later youm hatch and scamper

all over the Great Reef
yourm eggs in East Java, in the Coral Sea
off Bolong Beach in Zamboanga
with hawksbills
to the Philippines, nesting on yourm islands
of Tasmania, from Mexico across the Pacific
from Southern Russia to scatters south
yourm home's tropical, subtropical, liminal

in yourm deepest tessera
find that quiet crevice
please
don't drown in the nets!
but youm can't hold the air when youm're stressed
youm might sleep under time for hours at a time

and hum quietly into the confluence
to the heaviness
gaze up, beyond the surface
youm awake to the equatorial trail
Then, following yourm primordial thirst

yourm image dissolving into cerulean
push it away, pushing away,
youm gently sway, pushing it away
parting the curtains with yourm tender scalpels
pricks in a vast, murky membrane
by the firmament—these, yourm
yourm throat's feathers fanned
beside albatross
beside seals
to drown in the sun
Or youm clamber onto coast

Western Clownfish

clouds swim, sleepy, lazy like
milky mantas while
youm poise, fixed or shifting
nestled in yourm flubbering, flittering
in & out of yourm flubber pipes
so active, aggressive, clowning
flubbering, fighting out
or ducking, flittering about &
eyeing, defiant
and stingly
coupled up and a wee one
fashion plate, chase
yourm ghost beneath the spray
shoot back to the shudder realm
have another go, attack massive
the largest courage hurtling
down the death line
then moon tense, fuck lust
chase, bite, steer and
jiggle the vertical, chase to the nest
make memorable mists
drop yourm thousand eggs
on coral or rock, or next
to the sting
guard them until they break
larvae sinks to the benthic
but then they rise, a wobble
in the succulence of plankton
and float along the flux
until youm settle to the bottom
all yourm hearts in bulbs
like dice lying awake

youm hatch between creases of colour
but for streaks of yolk and yourm eyes
then youm blossom
orange-striped pearl, bold cod-
orange bulb, into big
chin, bright, white-
striped orange
black-stripped thin, thicker
inches of brilliant
and viable fruit
to learn a strict hermaphroditic
hierarchy: man becoming
woman, becoming largest
woman's rule, making eggs until death
when another man becomes her
and another readies for sex
yourm whole story is given to such otherness
youm pray for yourmself as others
and for yourm demise, yourm untamed animal
that charges at difference
that chases it from its own home
yourm silent songs of selection
yourm search for the gaze of exaltation
the rest becomes boring without it
—glance of the big, where are you?

scents connect, host lust
demand home dance, dance
dip yourm fins
in its tentacles, sweep
yourm whole being
through, mulch
yourm mucus coat
anemonefish becomes anemone
pinned by desire, by sweet pain
a wriggling cerebellum
a wriggling full of sting and symbol

heteractis magnifica, stichodactyla gigantea
a grin to fill the entrails of a killer
being prey is yourm purpose
youm bump heads with teeth
chase brittle stars, wrasses
and damselfish, flex bright muscle
to feed home, then come home
to clean it, to fan it with yourm fins
home's the dearest psyche, but it's angry
in a wisp of scythe, home
numbs yourm hide with stinging pipes
but if the venture's too long
or youm scrape yourm coat
youm will be stung by those nematocysts
yourm vigil could become death hiss

stingers rustle like silent chaperons
in perpetual winds, they thirst
for impermanence, youm drink
territory, chase snakes
down narrow rifts while a
small monster keeps falling
into molten delirium
a star is perpetually gargling
in a slowly swaying galaxy
pairs hiding in the Pacific warm
in sheltered reefs and lagoons, pairs
across the Indian, off Australia, through south-east Asia
the tongues of so many cities, smiles of so many houses, youm nibble
what the home discards, gobble up
copepods, isopods, zooplankton
and all the algae
youm would enjoy pure safety
in yourm rubbery oscillations
but for us, the long legs
who tank youm with the wrong stingers
chop yourm lives in half

youm don't care what god is
a tall wave can drown the galaxy
courage or peace, the coral's flame
is resolute
forever ready, nothing comes near
no-thing near home
cricks of fatigue and fertile delusions
pass through youm, restless pilgrims
wandering over plains
of swirling, vociferous grass

Shallow Estuary

transition-place, land-sea place where freshwater / meets and mixes with salt yourm / tidal culture protec
by peninsulas / Holocene history, a river-eroded / or glacially scoured valley / flooded with rising seas the
a brackish body with an opening / creeks flowing / a free connection to the ocean / a dynamic system with
diluted sea / the shocked river system

bar-built, lagoonish / by barrier beaches and barrier spits / yourm
plain / on a stable tectonic edge / marginal coast of minimal tide / offshore banks built by sand and wave
shore, sediment remade / into bounty, into overwash flats and dunes / the mainland ridge engulfed, shal-
shore currents, the spits / swelling with the littoral swerve

a dense salt wedge tunnels towards land, slips

most productive region, youm produce more / matter than jungle or farm
the unique communities of yourm tidal shelters / safe spawning places, sea
nurseries / migratory birds rest, refuel on fish and invertebrates / youm
control or conform / to the shifts in salt concentration / osmoregulators
osmoconformers / animals burrow from predation / thrive in stable precipitate
where bacteria drink oxygen / from that anoxic dross, its limited flux / what's
more important than phytoplankton?—liquid writing flushed out by the tides
its turbid cursive, abundant / diatoms and dinoflagellates in the sediment
(so much food is detritus / from the settlement of the sedimentation)

the kids walk down to yourm beach
hot footpaths burning their feet
I skim a slate and while it sinks
huge boats are lifting youm to the sky
so we lie together on yourm dry shallows
perfectly warm, perfectly still, by
yourm mangroves, swamps and rocky features
yourm fresh and saline marshes, yourm mud
flats, sand flats and sandy beaches
yourm deltas, tidal pools and marine grasses
compared with most youm welcome more
yourm precious plant buffers absorb
floods and surges, protect upland habitat
and our valuable real estate
estuarine plants and marsh grasses
translate craft back to shoreline

our dik-
our overfish
record of the An
the rest at rest in be-
seeping into yourm spec
furans, phenols, dioxins an
condition: plastics, pesticides
these contaminants, yourm cont-
runoff from impervious carparks
industrial discharge, construction se-
sewage from failing septic tanks
of fertilizer and pet waste from lawns, raw
is valuable filtration
of fresh silt, yourm performance
to eutrophic temper, ripple, flow
youm are that most productive habitat, tend-

unravelled by the tide
cords of upland exiles
begins where rhythms collide
riverine with maritime, yourm touch
Perform valuable transition, condition

-ted / by lanky barrier islands
bays, the harbours, the sounds
connection / to tide rhythm, the

narrow coastal inlets / on a gently sloping
/ deposited in stretched bars / parallel to the
low lagoons / glazed after flood, here come the long-

friction into wave / or surge overwhelms river, subsuming freshwater into / mixture

estuary: aestu-/ arium: tidal inlet of the sea, from aestus: semi-
to dilution, to sleep, sleep no more / morning salutation, eye
sleep no more / on yourm bed, spindly ocean / curling la-
cut away the deep / trembling or sleek, old skin is shed

yourm eutrophication and hypoxia
ing and damming
-ing, -grazing and wetland filling
-thropocene, our deforestation
nthic serenity
-ies' tissues
d heavy metals

engulfed by yourm own impulse / yourm stretch-
sense returns along the passage of flesh / youm
and forest / yourm secret net of form / stre-
limpid laughter in the shallows / what u-

an emergent morse, a series / of cl-
gabbled, bubble-bold, shine dr-

emporary

diment

ing

what's essential is
dissolved oxygen and variations
of salinity through space
what can be missed
is the sediment of settlement
in intertidal mudflats, erasing all space
for vegetation, clogging
mouths, gills

or excess oxygen feeds
excess life, which decays, devours
oxygen, produces
hypoxic and
anoxic zones

over a mind that holds firm against the onshore
that frantic, frivolous film
sheen of yourm absolute
of a quivering prism upon the shivering
toward being, the trend
but within youm everything vanishes: gestures
from yourm flat array
perhaps a tuft of knotted scrub rises precariously
perhaps a kelly brow, perhaps a slender island

enclosed tide, free to open
-lid of evening / sleep is dead
ke, ache no more / as yourm fables
/ sleep no more on yourm turbid bed

ed swing curdles to turrets / of invisible speed but
sigh with human necklace, with villages / of thunder
aked onto thought / what use sight if it should melt / yourm
se memory covered / in estuarine silt?

ues, petrified pulses, soaked echoes gobble-
ibbled still / echoes of ceaseless movement in low tide's parchment / yourm bony islands'
drying scalps (there's a hawk's foot
lofting the flats, an old wreck gnawn
down to vertebrae)

youm grant small creatures like the eye
the skill to live by water, which is never still
yourm key's a quiet retreat
a seethe, slowly sinking back into position
without ever leaving: yourm wrinkled veil
over a timorous moon, its quavering
axons bending into drift
a brain smooth as ground reef
a billowing phrase receding into the green
splayed over a continent's shelf

Mangroves

through slops of mud, mud-
lobsters slouch, crabs
munch leaves, seedlings, make mulch
for the mangal, this dark
and sloppy ballroom:

youm breed sediment

in Tamil Nadu, in Vietnam
Thailand and the Philippines
in Cambodia's Kompong Sammaki, youm produce

shorebirds nest with crab-
those ish, rawns and ails
galaxies in yourm pockets
forest, souls of countless
coastal rainforest, sea of forest, salt

this rule:
no breath without yourm pithy pillars
chart of charts of sacrifice
monotonous mangal no revolution of day
into days

we threaten youm more than most:

of beige jellyfish
places, collect bits
scavenge metals still the swells to build

for hotels, for shrimp farms
though we've removed most
for the cans thrown into yourm forest
youm confront the ocean, translate it
fish, crustacean, coastline

youm blossom for the fruit bat
above urtles, izards and fishing cats
monkeys, proboscis monkeys

algae and barnacles gather
around yourm quiet feet
where sponges anchor
and feed
and the bruised nails of oysters
cut the soles of shoes

firstly, yourm charcoal genius, then
hotels steal yourm mosquito chatter
we kill light, cough smog
youm sink sewage, toxic seepage
pesticides and herbicides, crude oil clogs
youm lenticels

yourm remains span the planet
saline coastal tropical sub-tropical

youm sip brackish fluid
super-briny fluid concentrated
by evaporation, youm are
woody, specialised, youm thrive on the edges
the brackish lands between fish and plants
between bodies and constellations

star fixed on the chin of the sky
yourm stilled mind
exposed to the sway
of saline mangal, shrubland coastal
yourm fine judgements, organic contents
stalls of aquatic beats
withdrawing in the rush

boiled and desiccated in the low
flooded with salt in high tide
thinnest niche

warm   sheltered shorelines
estuarine, packed
into deltas of large Asian rivers
sludgy, swampy places
where low tide shows yourm

an out-
of spectres surveying
great cities of spires
into gnarled trunks
chunky arteries rise

of salinity, of temperature
most motley moistures, broadest spectrum
yourm scrawny, most porous ontology
then flooded and cooled once more

roots rise from the brain
hunting for the membrane
for aerial lanes, pneumatophores
soil straws, rubbery
wooden axons covered
in lenticels, poking their thin
knobby conks with oyster
dragon's teeth shell callouses, stilt
prop, snorkel or peg type
knee, ribbon or plank type
breathing roots, buttresses
and above-ground roots, knee and
ribbon and buttress combinations
at the base, roots
full of aerenchyma
roots as stilts, as support
going tide as negotiators between tree & sea
aerial roots and tap roots filter out the salt
roots snake around with the upward loops,
rising from the brackish weaves, their
ferreting endings, incessant willows woven
and reedy, needy needles, weedy
thoughts scratched through salt

impervious to verge
youm explode like a nova, like a trauma
wanding magically from fidgeting structure
youm taught termites that essence must
shatter, twenty feet of splintered
skeleton
youm speak as a fountain speaks

but youm diverge

dropped root
youm reached for sludge
through months and months
through dormancy
through desiccation
travelling tirelessly
synthetic sustenance
ready to go, photo-
propagated propagules
viviparous
and froth dots
sun dots
on home currents
germinating seeds
millions of years ago
and flowed west
where youm proliferated
in south-east Asia
mangal mecca's

hangers, bottles & tyres
fishing out coat
James Cameron saw yourm limbs
tubular piles, the art's apart from either
squiggling, mounting
with yourm revolving shadow
naming the afternoon
youm loom in packs
and stinging sunlight
to anaerobic soils
to salinity, to inundation
convergent in yourm solutions

scales of names, their numbers
a column of noon and
into zodiac and solar arrow
its condensation doubles into zodiac
of evaporating, scarlet plasma
their claws frame a wall
the soggy blades, land spirits
the weight of law on yourm lashes
crystal crusts on grey leaves
the cusp of mangal
above and below

perception ever

in zonations
yourm multiplying adaptations
expand swamp sanity, fertile tones
speckled and sluggish
propped above the low with stilt roots

bottle ottle blottle lottle   blink lack blind bog   blurrp blirrup blottle

youm won't listen to sodium, or youm store it
in vacuoles, in beards
of floury crystals
which youm shed like early drafts
shrink stomata
strain yourm salty sap

pneumatophores, or
so youm turn to the atmosphere with
methane and sulphides, kill yourm loam
soluble iron, inorganic phosphates
bacteria free nitrogen
hard to find but anaerobic
food's yourm biggest problem / oxygen's

poking, the unsettled levels lungfuls through bark
youm fish for oxygen, drag it under
exclude sodium with

at least three senses:
the mangrove forest
the mangrove swamp
and mangrove forest biome

the habitat
the entire plant assemblage
the mangal
all trees and large shrubs
in the mangrove swamp
the family
youm feed on iron, store gases at yourm sources
silently, the grim consoler
of sulphur tears, conducting
at low ebb, carefully

ultrafiltration

youm came to English from Spanish
via Portuguese
origins in Guaraní
mangled into grove
mangle
mangue
mangrow

about 110 species of mangroves

in the sense
that a tree grows
in a saline swamp

but only a few are
rhizophora

the trees of the genus rhizophora
the rhizophoraceae

like red mangrove, rhizophora mangle

red mangroves, rhizo-, rhizo-

Sand-bubbler Crab

youm burrow
beneath the wet
world, which recedes
for yourm emergence,
scour history, suck food from
bulging pellets
work radially
from yourm entrance
yourm complex patterns
of little lodes, balls
littering beaches
inflated pellets posed
for disintegration
youm mesmerise
with a hasty, delicate art
an artist flees, fleeting arrays crum-

on sandy banks in the tropical
Indo-Pacific, the immediate
superimposed semantics
an abundant inheritance
of leaf, lid, seed, a crafty
dweller, widespread
in the Daintree, on Magnetic Island from across the artful oceans down and down the

balled-up grit
configurations
snack remnants
and briny sparkle glinting
with mineral, this
language dragged
from the underground, the polished molecule the content shickled with sun

sand
bubbler
sand bubb
ler sand bub
bler sand
bubbles and bubb
led sand bubble
sand bubbler sand bubblers
and bubbles and bubb
led sand

youm can't see
yourm completion
the bank's
yourm outside, borrowed
between tides
to scrawl, sculpt signs for higher eyes

ble wash away as the tide rises rinses fuels yourm next pursuit

coast

youm sculpt the shore
into an image
of the under, of what
the over
will become,
brown, sugary
micro-reef
and lake smear
the secret
ether dries
into art
complicates
all constructs, yourm motionless eruptions stare surround before

distinct form
linked with
other forms, a
communication
a notion of
communication
a notion
a communication is being
proffered
a form, a line
forms, lines in repetition a fact imposed upon another (what ink? what paper?)

an archive
reduced to
tracks, track
to spheres
sphere to
damp granules, yourm
geometric poetics
asemic practice
arrangements of deep
logic, of literary
output I'm not
equipped to
decode
this poethical
reposition, splayed ecocentrism

like a cat
with wings
a composition
that spills
that stars
then fills
as youm move
back in along a tendril
of intention
towards where
and for what
the semantic
implication of a swarm
choked with vi-
brations, biotic and abiotic components entering into bodies their capacity to write

complete submission before yourm hours of repose

sprawled
like continents
yourm thoughts
bulge before
youm drop them
and pass each one
through yourm tiny scrum
to where they rest
and dry into a wedge
of yourm melody
a bevy of slick
pixels, slicked
up beads
pebbled bells
pocked and
dotted, grey
fades for pale
coffee for bleeding
clay, split
static flats
fleshed into fractured

the turn leaves
behind a leathery
smoothness
in which youm
chisel frames
of crystalline scratch
the terrain recalled
in the completion
of circumference, the
fine atoms of dot
sculpture built
into the clumped
brain of a silt reef
patterned in parts
by the tide's own
script, yourm lines
laced across
carved warnings, yourm
squallform as inlet
force, escape as scuttle
parched clock, when
crunched strata meet dried lumens, sug-

circumferences, which begin to pile to fuse into mild mounds all this patter-pill painted lake spill peb-

arced bound to blur yourm capable agents yourm communication

what youm
consume
has a low concentration
of organic matter
is concentrated
by egestion
of indigestible matter
all excess balled
overhead, discarded

to think of
this string
of pearls
wet dirt
eggs, slopped
balls kicked out
to dry, a trail of droppings catching light

yourm art
is to spread
without spreading
gest pearl balloons with scrapped pasts
to produce fissures
without being seen
from here youm talk
bles of smoke
within the folded visible
translating the core's
simmer into cooling
freckles on yourm
moist surface
where it begins
to breathe again
in the low tide's lore
the larger, greasy-caramel blobs framed by a straight

when it consumes yourm vision a remarkable remainder

bubblers of
muggle munch
kicking clicker
filter of the genera
scopimera and dotilla
of the family
dotillidae, slight
across the
carapace, characterised
by a gas window on the merus of the legs

this advice, these
yourm brief friends, the
time, the energy
the production
of the masterpiece
the expert sculptor
the crabbiest, a bit
aloof, easily irritated
yourm diminutive slips
from burrows
to scour the radius
for debris, youm scurry
simultaneously, as if
each were at the ends
of a net which
if I only think of movement, is suddenly retracted by a hand beneath the earth

youm slit
dotted still
ness with exiguous
cracks of fi
dget, sift
and sculpt
soft spectra
thread
ed
with highlights, how
youm with scant
measure
of the turn decide
to lay down
yourm selves like this
for some of
that once living
however scant
its praise, and when
I move, youm race li-

line beside which lies a pie slice of smaller pebbles pied off again by a groove by a whip across another ke a hyphen into nothing

pebbled pie effervescent sculptures in proportion to yourm sizes

Fireflies

flashing, ~~unphotic~~
sex
yourm powder snaps flux
into photos

yourm spells
echo yourm names
souls ask where to
go ghost says no

burrow
under
in spri-

light loves luciferase
~~on the~~ lucifern
magnesium
~~and~~ oxygenated
steroids trap
sour trap poison

~~mitts~~ flicker
in womb
erratic insect
systematics

mangroves inhale
~~with~~ heaving glow
synch*ron*ised emiss*ions*
of spontaneous order, kelip-

kelip a*long* Malaysian rivers
totonbala*gon* through the Philippines, thousands

all year in the town of *Don*sol

the luminous poetics
of snap language
home
bark, rebound
ng

sprites leak
from ~~yourm~~ surface
ecru-bodied larvae
elytra leathery

a lover ~~strewn~~
upon a bed of wings
youm feed
on nectar on pollen
or never

how sonancy becomes
stage how night
is a cry
shout yourm horrid taste

in the between ~~sex~~
slips ~~like~~ a flag, dripping
larvae's grooved mandibles
inject slugs with numbing
fluid and feed

larvae feed
snails in C-

~~micro~~ beasts wrapped
in silver floss yourm

pulsating clumps blink
~~new~~ morse collapse

geometries
into ~~throb~~ code
the organ in yourm
abdomen names youm
with near-heatless light

desire turns ~~white~~
~~and fondles~~ the noun

youm croon in marshes in slimy
woods with food

for yourm larvae—light-
babies, glow worms—youm grow

to flight but sometimes
females are flight

less

broad days ~~fade~~
like a lie

on larvae on
uba

no infrared ~~or~~ ultra-
violet lexicon, chilled

yellow, willow, pallid-rose ~~or~~ silver
from the lower abdomen

winged beetles lightning
bugs lampyridae
in the coleopteran
conspicuous crepuscular use
of luminous cognition

~~millions of~~ nerve
tips thrashing ~~out~~
~~their~~ fervour
the femme-fatale mimics lightning
to attract and devour meandering males

~~yourm~~ whisper trees
their stirred evening
yourm crawling, ebullient belly
streaks of lithe wanting
through night for a few

hundred lives brands
yourm brief passage
of continuous couple chase

yourm urgent
~~fringeless~~ origin, jet
engulfs the vertical
hashed motifs
of optical epics

Gecko

Bengali takshak

took, took, *tore*! yourm call

muffled rooster

Javenese tokek   Filipino tuko   tokkae in Malay a mating   croak, token, gekk-gekk   or pookay

for sex   for music, for   defence   yourm fatidic voice   disturbs concerts of   insects   rubber

fuck-   you, fuck-you, Ameri-   cans in Vietnam, plucked   plastic guitar   froggy quack or   weeny

took two
  took two
    monkey chuckle, cackle!

saw, zook ball
  zook! baaall
    nearly chook talk, buzz saw

cackle
  squelching stutter, squeaking tick
    song snake
      tubby soul!

cylindrical, squat, robust
youm compress contented
ugliness
granulate velvet
defend against
malevolence
fleck yourm spots
of yellow and blush, or toffee-
coloured, tailed by a chalky thumb
a breathing twig
or coffee sticky as a skinny slug
tooking little knot
toffee slips across the wall

youm lighten, darken
to blend, youm cast
no shadow on a trunk
open yourm skin to the bark
erase yourm mark, vanish
in form, a brief sniff
and shiver
the temper of the void, the vertical

yourm pupil's bistre
to greened-bistre, orange or
black, those gelatinous beads,
fused, transparent
lids, a third
eye's on top of yourm head

fingers of squashed setae
cling to speed, suppress
gravity, youm taste
air, scent ray
discard yourm tail for thrashing, semi-
prehensile deviation

gekko gecko
nocturnal arboreal gecko
painted by jungle and cliff *gecko*
yourm noggin poking from a rotten stump
yourm orbit becoming urban *gecko*
yourm stripped fields
hunted tuko medicinal tuko *gecko*
bright pet tuko
youm flicker between st asis *gecko*
youm move in hidden flicker floo
youm tell that step by curl
by fanning measure there's no
gecko here no / gecko here!

yourm brightest eyes search
for the rising pyre

a bend a slept bend
light concentrated

refracted
by subcutaneous aperture

brilliance becomes more
from obscurity { than its source

the night mimes yourm tail
the insistent explorer

turn gravity to where youm want it
muscular jaws)   throw it into sound
(we know yourm   youm sprout from
laughing at apes   cracks and frames
a monkey ventriloquy   freeze in sight
a room full of calls   but dart at slight-
the tiniest shapes   est shift
is the nervous homebody   youm wax spectral
bear human initials
youm are the seer
of what seems
of the puffed parentheses
youm roam walls and ceilings
trawling the night for prey
ambling by / others fly
youm crush their casings, munch them down
shoot for dark before
returning forever to calm
dimpled slopes
turn gravity to where youm want it
cook it into sound

so terri
torial
yourm
attack
any
thing
else in
yourm
terri
tory

soli
tary
lying
on
stone
always
alone
but for
mating

lay
yourm
hard
eggs
and
guard
them
with
vicious
til they
hatch

Magpie

a complex vocal array
a branch line scooting away
through the meadow
of beautiful pitch   such that   youm
suck   wind free
the octave/s
contracting to splendid mimic
or warble, the most Australian   musical
melodious
subs
pitched at low hertz nyaw   ing at the warble   nyaw
bodeebodowa-aba falling
into the ether
after breeding
then carolling's a   louder music
defends yourm   plot   a flared   cleft
loops into grass with more
with elements   with nyaw
bodeebodowa-aba
nyawbodeebodowa-aba
hoaaal-yeebodwa-aba
are youm watching   slur the indistinct
titling back yourm head   expand
yourm chest
beak brushes red
hoaaal-yeebodawawa-aba-aba
coolawarlyouboudafinda
pines turn tender   over
gwarklewarbledoyeebaw-ay
and quardleoodleardlewardle
yourm flapping wings say
yourm carolling   before dawn
(a dawn song)
yourm dusk yarn
(a dusk song)   clap beaks
or shoot high hertz
depending on eagles or monitors

collect
specific epithet, coracias
tibicen in the Port Jackson
region, Latin's tibicen, a flute's melodious
vernacular, a piping roller, local Eora
and Darug names, tarrawonnang, djarrawunang
wibung, marriyang, booroogong and garoongong
are Wiradjuri, carrak's Jardwadjali,
among the Kamilaroi, burrugaabu, galalu, guluu
then flute-bird, maggie, bird of organs and bells
further out youm're warndurla on Yindjibarndi dirt
black-backed, white-backed western hybrids
with hybrid grey or striped backs, four
black-backed races split / a scion
its splinter, a coracias tibicen tibicen
a nominate form, Moreton Bay to Victoria
coastal or near coastal, restricted to east

gold brown or wine
rock white raven eyes
a bill's solid wedge
solid wedge-shaped bluish-
white and slate dipped
in paint worn
off at the tip a little
hook at the tip
a bulb sliced bled
white a sculpture pierced
flooded with ink glossy
dusk statue fragment
between tree fragments
youm're air aren't air
a currawong a cooling
valve plucking
scad solid sturdy
long and strong legs yourm
tail has a black terminal band

nest is a platform a bowl
of twigs and wire
an interior intellect
of grass and hair
nest is early spring
nests incubate eggs
feed those infants when
so many die
in those first dire months
then umans in-

but youm can fight
for terrain for years
so much is spent / fighting
mobbing
various opponents various attacks / a raptor's
a sentinel's rallying call
to live is to fight, slim party
or carolling's a signal
of ownership of warning a negotiation two of the most
dominant parade
the border fluff and carol while the rest stand watch
or a show of collective strength
a row at the border, an aerial display
swoop dive a call to warn
but manus flutter's a submissive display
primary feathers flutter

vade
prompt low, fast
flying, clacking
alarm calls and swoops
snaps, pecks, dive
bombs
pecking at the eyes
a boy killed in traffic
while evading a swooping pie to six weeks
so much is done to defend those four

across the grass youm walk
with hands in pockets
bounce feet or
careful stepping tippy-toes
tilted heads / youm stroll and talk
or stand to watch and
then youm launch
into dream, grawl-
-pinge-ndanatotherow
wa-alberderg-ordargodee-
hear me finally a kite a those
tiniest people / yourm neck's
scaly velvet sheen
yourm grounded
fall lawn patrol
roll over and explose yourm belly afternoon strolls away
to dissolve in bark

ventures into homes to beg
umans
or paces the open methodically sedentary language, poems
eating each a lot of magpies poke the sky
invertebrate omnivorously diurnally, or throw songs

the worms, pedes, ails and iders
the roaches, nts, eetles and oths
go skinks, ice, ogs
go grain, figs, walnuts and tubers
flip the ane toad

gorge on the under

the larval tones, the vibrations
smaller prey swallowed whole
youm rub off the stinger
before swallowing the wasp
yourm bill probes the earth

youm're brash, cocky
an Australian psyche

youm tug at stuff, pick at it
give it to others, fly off with feathers
while yourm mates give chase

youm tackle, jump, mock
fight / youm play
with blue-faced eaters of
honey and pipits

youm are born with the land in yourm throat
with the blood of nightmare
awakening the Yindjibarndi
signals for sunrise in the Pilbara
of groups or flocks or fringes

at the night

absent only from the densest
forest from arid
deserts youm forage
the open youm own
the outback's
scattered remains

a male and a female
rule a tribe and feast on bounty
but the younger and the frailer
make larger flocks and drift
like dirty, tattered clouds
in search of water

Stray Cat

/

covered in fleas and ear mites

of Jerusalem, lean, not skeletal

Canadian Parliamentary Cats, youm

in Rome's Colosseum, like

in droves but youm that grow can thrive

yourm young die

We brought youm rats and mice / for 5000 years in China / felis sylvestra lybica we left youm / to viruses and leukaemia / flea-anaemic full of coccidia of giardia / stuffed with worms of tapes and hooks / recurring diarrhoea / dogged by dehydration infections / in yourm thorax yourm thatching / of thin bone sucked / of flesh by our disdain.

Curling creature / cooler than loam curled / around shrubs around posts / the colours of cultures of clothes / at infinite speed or gelid / in the gloaming into the gutters / or the corners of dimensions with talk / in tongues or chins space condenses / inside youm and springs / into fur.

  youm know where to look, exactly
where to look:
          1) seeing
        the shape change
    youm charge at residues of light, or
                              2) without resentment youm race
                                                  like a tiny comet
                                                        into the dark:

where youm hesitate, drag nourishment to a crevice / to live on what would kill us

gulp, paw and shiver

entries and exits

yourm kittens prod at the ulcers

around yourm nipples

around columns, walls

youm punctuate with lick, coagulate grammar

yourm seamless passage, its endless day

with a patter or a side rush

moody-

shadowy

a purchase on trees, obviously

on a continuum youm are continuum, a ball of breeze

scavenger

of odents, abbits and eptiles

killer, moon-clawed mauler

of sodden scraps

~~youm peel back jungle~~

beneath parrot racket, prickling in the shade

~~beneath their cheats of flight and all-sight~~

their green, switching songs

~~youm hold yourm scarred head steady~~

and creep through yourm mind's thicket

~~of waving, ashen bamboo~~ until,

youm ask / the spirits of yourm purchase, the spirit that wakes youm / and the
to the night. "What's / happening?"
incomprehensible voice which / speaks
eternal idol youm are becoming / the
fill yourm lungs and howl / drawing on the
make it understood that youm are sacred / youm
from deep / in yourm chest the raucous cry / youm
youm do not recognise / a single smell / forcing out
them not to forget yourm face / in a tunnel where
lords / to disappear when they near / or to beg
is this / to live wide-eyed before the ancient
swer note with glassy note / what life
us / dirty and dishevelled / youm an-
hiss and growl unless youm trust
wounds in mating fights / youm
of dried ice / youm die from
spits that dissipate in burls
urst into sandy hiss /
urm throat / to b-
and rises in yo-
into a globe
from the abyss of yourm being, *rage* boils

most beautiful spirit of all / the one that meows and purrs and resembles youm / they have all disappeared

Where are youm now?
If youm feel gently with yourm paw
youm find nothing.

There's nothing anywhere.

crooning eager, mouwling
nouwling over specks of kitten squeak
yourm elegant skeleton weaves
between a touch and the tip of contact
between vista and vision cut by a blink
yourm strung, snaking lines
yourm language dribbles over lines
or surges from the depths of a curl
mauw, how, nowling
youm talk upwards or outwards, obstinately
ostensibly friendly, through in a whisk
youm talk to a form
or its fancy
taken up by the wind

youm toy with rubbish, stop
for sauce on a scrapped wrapper, bowlsey
wolsey, gorgeous ploddy
puno squibblet, yourm every movement
is a delight, youm push the serious
into impromptu skits
youm know this is true, truly: no act
sound or area is beneath youm
no speed or theorem above

cool as a sun, youm snooze
in midday's zoom of flies
youm could sleep anytime/where, it's
yourm waiting, youm're
always happy to be woken

youm mask yourm art in long pink yawns
in pits of fur, gloved paws
and stretches
but when a fat slither
skitters through leaf litter
youm are feral muscle, a signal's
lightning crystalline
as strike! all thought's
packed into claws
that once were hidden

our languid habitation
which never cease to resist
through yourm succulent lenses
a wisdom we catch glimpses of
that orbits yourm tenement
the boundless encephalon
the whole province or none of it
tubers crossing from cheeks into spectrum
musing with yourm slender, articulate pole
over birds' antics
in the afternoon youm tiredly preside

and become momentary
where youm and I might coalesce
many continue alone
some emerge to play, where
a pool of swirling relation, where
but nothing's as true as what youm wish for
of things before they arrive
as they close, yourm knowing
of yourm truth in the eyes
colossal, the proof
my presence is clumsy
next to yourm precinct
/
and youm are lapping at the afterlife's cold milk
on Time
into that nanosecond when we stumble
breaking sideways
like a diminutive wave forever
folded under another
of sleep at noon, one wrist
to the impervious peace
delirious drooling
from ludicrous clowning
or the irreverent is incessant
yourm quest for the delicate

in those plodding buds

Eastern Whipbird

as unpeeling fog, swollen leaning— / toooooo—
silence speared, the only sound alive
hip-yeeeeeeee—
splices presence, presents hip-
ohhhhhhhh—
the call, the feeler call, heeeeeere (or)
the wisp winds through, heee-heee—
bends like an eel, the purest song
whistle builds
the eastern call, the long

magpies weave their nets of rope
youm survey tangled undergrowth
by pale barked pipes, in woods
pushed from the city, siren
of the East, dwarfed by silence only,
youm stalk thickets where

an infinite sheet of indigo
spring in a shrub, yourm need waiting
youm fossick in ground litter
and dense scrub near waterways
to Victoria, Australia's
in the rainforest margins, the damp gum stands

bull ants crawl across baked strips

circles concentrating upon one another / heeeee—eee— / phooooo— a loud-

yourm figure flees forward
to pat the shining bellow
to draw its gasp, flutters
across compass, nominate
olivaceus, structure
uplifts the streak into white
the cheek, the neck, chest's

flaps in the wind slate with patchy, streaky white
crested black

nibbling on sects and brates olive back, darker
wings, tail, green

clammy littoral band grass coat
from Queensland

—wit!
the floor—jou!
yourm barrel spikes
a sharpened huff—ziou!
all / flushed with jet—zwat!
a wall / a sharp whip distinct from
slugged whip JOOOLP / a whip against
anthem hurtling / splits forest / THIS ZONE
expansion home / shot through the gully / I-AM brazen
crack shooting back sucked / back, woit! / or forward with hooped
ringing whip / an explosive whip- / crack the precise coordination / the familiar whip-

a tree fern's warm ochre eyes
yourm pale marble eyes
watching within the angles
into the upper, frumpy frowner
the lower beak pressed
neck and a needle beak
jutting rudder screened by scrub, bright snowy
yourm mohawked scruff
sedentary, but seen me youm fly away
far less than heard, on seeing

the instant pair, the antiphone
  the shiny, salient tchew-tchew
    the lantern lands, a small applause, jou-jou-

jou! youm bounce out
  laser fire, Star Wars
    zap, the blast

through the stillness, the smashed glass chew-
  chew! riding
    yourm minor apocalypse

feed alone, in pairs or groups, a breeding pair
occupies a territory, defends it year-round
youm make a cup of sticks
and bark lined with fine grasses
and hide it near the ground
to incubate broods of bodiless sounds

an imagination gazing through the paperbarks
youm are home's invisible sign
resonance of a form without frame

but how to sing
without a body?
a territory's a body, a low orb
secluded by cumulus where silence
is found, its nervous textures sensed
where youm enter
into matter, a tone
larger than its basis, an anchor
a ghost icon
spirit choir, the Eastern pulse

too shy for a centre
threaded through hearts
a spirit hymn

strong as a taste or a shape
yourm liquid location
its memory, its confirmation

Pinatubo Volcano

1991, the century's biggest eruption   tens of thousands of evacuations   before Typhoon Yunya

before 1991 youm hadn't spoken   since much of our memory began   yourm ancestor emerged

blooming, chopped lake   outline on the inside of yourm   impression great   petrified hands linger mixed a lethal cocktail   of ash and rain and youm destroyed   yourm plot with flows of ash and

millions of years   ago Ancient   Pinatubo calmer Pinatubo   a lone peak a somma volcano   its

liquesce   below, the reverie of poetry   balances on yourm beating   crux, crushed rim hear the magma redrew rivers with manic strokes, there youm came wishing, then youm turned you-

remnants strewn through yourm rugged skirt youm're surrounded by chunks of its caldera by

impending hull of geologic addling yourm idle pursue a cause in a play of stacks youm rise rm head and said   the Lord of the Event   was angry with illegal loggers   with the National Oil

plugs and domes of the eroded   somma / born beneath the mesh of its   pyroclastic membrane

from the womb towards the solitude   of word's shelter   erode become inconspicuous obscured

Company who probed and drilled youm for geothermal heat wishing yourm heart into stra-

yourm plasma factor slowing to rigid youm arose tropical priest! thirty-five thousand years ago

by thick jungle filled with Itas, hunting/whispering people people of wheat and rice and barley ngest country   why   prevent the stream dam   or stop it in vowel?   magma was filling yourm

in time's most cataclysmic explosion   Inararo, phosphor thawed   to a pyre five   times larger than

of animal and volcano   who fled the low   to escape the Spanish   monsoons seduce yourm soils summit   youm shook, domed   huge with lava   and burst   amazed the sky with yourm   roar-

’91   this is life: to wake   up episodically, violently   spew yourm massed innards   over the low

birth   lush circumference   absorb the sopping bliss before   yourm scorched midday yourm excing verb   lashed whips of pyroclastic juice   shot new lightnings   yawned friction in yourm uprus-

the Sacobia   the Pasbul the Crow   youm scream for decades for   centuries but all   the while

eeding   drain, titian striations and strains   of settlement yourm   deep sentiment   Pinatubo, ferthing ash   youm raged for one day   unleashed   earthquakes   tephra falls of dacite   hornblende

youm shrink   as yourm unwelded   deposits erode   as youm destroy yourm viscous   domes

ile place place   where crops grow   'made to grow' in Sambal   a stratovolcano   in the uplands and plagioclase, anhydrite youm rivered in Yunya's typhoon swallowed a lake which boiled

youm let pressure go by, sailing unsold until Buag when youm went back slept beneath rai-

of Cabusilan separating west from east on the island of Luzon andesite and dacite discouwith acid   until a deluge coded   it frigid   youm split with landslide   yourm greyed blood loose

nforest creep beneath Ita   sunk into gullies and ravines   the Ita know youm're living   stone

rse cool   lavas more viscous   than basalt pile up   in vents grow domes   some stratovolcanoes on yourm steep and gullied slopes   beside those youm killed with yourm scream   yourm loose tor-

junction of light and adumbration, abode   of the Lord of the Event   who smashed youm in a fight

are just piles of domes   coagulating along arcs   with little magma   with long, long periods of repso has flowed in rains   and killed many times that   number since o   maw of lake   sulphur nee-

pulverised yourm peak in fury   to teach us the power of fear   or there's Bacobaco   terrible sea

ose   but those lavas plug   up plumbing   gas bubbles up   from yourm innards into   explosive dle   piercing tract towards   a floret of anarchy and love   love   youm came, killer Christ   ever-

spirit   transformed into a huge turtle shouting   balls of flame   chased off by the spirit   hunters

rages of lava and pyroclastic   layers   youm might be more placid   than those large silicic caldera searching space for the   end of yourm self   all around youm, what's left?

to refuge inside youm   to shower the low with hot   rock and mirth   for three days   howling

complexes but still youm kill   more by inviting life   onto yourm slopes not   to mention yourm

the world trembled longly, Luzon
youm covered in darkness
sun undercut with a scrape, yourm
sodden ash blanketed Asia
with various vectors of chromatic
and fabric currents, traces
of terror, of a planetary explosion
youm belched billions of tonnes
of magma, sulphur and aerosol, shaped
a new atmosphere of sulphuric haze
youm vomited copper, chromium
nickel and zinc, cadmium
lead, mercury and arsenic
so loudly the planet shook coughed up dust, cooled the climate
for years yourm stratosp-
almost all pla-

steep piles of ash or yourm lava and domes soaked in monsoon shaken by earthquakes yo-

today youm dwell outside
we scratch about in yourm eyeball's liquid
shedding on the brink of somewhere else
unaddressed
unmappable

by degrees
heric acid lingered
nts were destroyed
when the Ita returned
most of their villages were destroyed
so most left, and lost youm, and their map

urm willingness to discard   whole flanks of yourm face   in a sector collapse

Tarsier

acute sense: distinct
auditory cortex, high hertz
poetics, the sigh
and the cry ride
the flux, shy
rainbow over weeks
of tiny cryptography, squeaky
creature code, a cry's ultrasonic
ellipse saddles the redux

far above the bounds
of my perception, coos
and calls beyond the uman
yourm secret social poetics: a lone tone
followed by shrills
nails-on-a-chalkboard trills
fluctuating above all facts
except whales' and dolphins'
and bats' and rats' and cats'

yourm complex, sexually dimorphic dawn / duet, before sleep (a short chirping
growing louder) (a snapped, descending / whistle) (tracks unroll in parallel)
(changes markedly / marked) a chirp, a chevron- / shaped call, a rapidly
modulated pitch, down-up / up-down, a female's eerie whistling /
jungle sonics / a male's clear upwards / downwards chevron-
shapes / a female's long, mournful whistle / a screeched
exhalation / youm constrict the larynx, brake air /
into rapid melodics, chop / and start speech
again aga- ag-

no tapetum lucidum
with ultrasonic yelps youm
spear darkness, its persistence
youm wait, disclose
yourm hollow sting, a half-
finished phrase, syntax gestating
spreading out in bulbous
comet, that primal
call compressing gaps

skeleton's squeezed primate,
wheeze while youm munch on moths
on butterflies like a bat, a poem
that dissolves, that dissipates
an ultrasonic corrosive
of location, an exclusive poem
no platoons of audience
youm hide children from death
or intercept the ultrahigh:

youm perk up at / insect chitchat / focus for kill

big-vision
largest eyes to body size
apprehension as reflection
an endless face
alien face

globe-eyed
brain as eye
sound into crystal
frog face
two peeled, gleaming grapes

balance yourm heavy head in silence / wait
in silence for prey / silently yourm cells
weave independent / primate lines

a small, shy hand
permanently shuddering
frightened that time or that it won't
in its dress of sable mantles
in this immense terrain
yourm rugged heart's half
of mine but whole, little wide-
eyed ball, twig light, slight as who
we were, as who we'll never be

fist squashed in tree fork
youm nuzzle into beige
and ochre velvet, cusp
of fuzz congealed in knuckle, ear,
rat's tail, an elderly
lady's hands with spidery fingers
like anemone flutes or ET sticks
with globed tips, knobbed
knuckles and mushroom-cap pads

son of sun, granddaughter / of daughters, tenement of temper / of what
could not be left out / youm remember essence and what it / does,
that this will be the last residence / yet youm are wonder-less,
thought-full / so much has happened already / so much
has pooled in the eyes, ruptured / the walls of recall

limbs of chicken wing, frog legs
frog ready, springy
elongated tarsi and fused
tibiofibulae send youm
vertical, clinging and leaping
yourm third finger's an upper arm
youm sprouted nails and four claws
yourm night laws, where primates
leap like insects

become insects
devour them
feast on petite flight and reptile
forage alone like yourm sleep
youm sit on human tongue-tip
yourm smallest foetus, our olden mind,
Yoda-wise, our yearning
collapsing at the end
of sight, yourm highest sermon

{ }

Satin Bowerbird

a bushed, shrouded lustre

along eastern and southern coasts

youm feed on fruits on

on ects when breeding

and leaves when wintry

the major cities

youm
complete all parts yourm art hangs
in strands the jade of the / flock olive as cat the olive over off-/ white and dark scalloping the da-

here youm come

minimally nomadic, nib-

from treetops down, sedentary or

surround

scatter through the rainforests

the open, the wet gum forests

the wetter woodlands, the rain-

forests of the Atherton Tablelands

rk / grey bill the bright lilac burl / the bright rush through the funnel / of the flow of sensation the

the old oanna dawdle

wary of the carpet ake, the forest at

luxuriate in early sun, forever

beats, youm

slow, deep, strong

swift, swooping

bling fruit

made
like a ready-
struct yourm / stage
marine socks / youm con-
flowers pegs and feathers / ultra-
drinking straws and bottle tops / shirts
of brown ails / yourm cobalt jewels / yourm
with the earth / opal streaks over the hearth / shells
cut leaves and turn / them over so the paler / sides contrast
every morning youm frame an arena / a frail frame a courtship arena

radiant document / the solitary mature the medium / sized glossy satin with volcanic / violet on art's

yourm other prompts jelly muscle jiggle / wobble a ritual displayed
postures and / colours swirl into refrains / bow strut quiver
yourm wings / mimic machines mechanical / rattle
buzzing and more / a decoration in yourm
bill the circle is dancing / a whirr of
painting navy splashed / with
wattle the whole / re-
frain is the be-
ing / wings
outstretched and quivering / the whole refrain is the being
of sensation

a complex aria of found and affect
in the song mine, the oldest objects
is scene
blue as love, art is what you see, what
what's that, blue boy, play boy?
into diffuse violet highlights
mass becomes satin ripple, coils light
chime above a beak of apical opal
yourm lamp's intense licks of lilac
full blue-black in yourm seventh year

or it swerves and collides with the leaves
pours over youm, seeps into youm
seal shape, sealed slick, light
youm build scene with yourm
black root, lure of scene
splayed azure from its sleek
yourm anatomy spills into art
pale beryl path
yourm complete art, yourm joy opera, noisy
and breeding, noisiest
in the bower's vicinity
the harsh grinding, the churring
and wheezy buzzing, not
meat synaesthesia but blocs
of sensation in the territory, the rapid
rollicking tzzarr-tzzarr-tzzarr-
tzzarrtz, tint, chopped
melodics and postures
yourm chaa-chaa-chaa
and schwitt-schwitt-schwitt, sketch a total art
whistled whitchiew, mimicked
thwack-static, chop chuckle, static chat, seductive
chuckle chitter, bricks of sonorous
refrains of boro-
leealal-qwark boroleealalqwark
or rough hiss, refrains
of posture and paint,

creates an entry, slices winter
with stage, yourm frame on stems
a building with décor
the parallel walls, waves
split into sticks
vegetable matter chewed into sticky
paint, youm maintain it all meticulously, all
year round, yourm stick church, its kindle
flaming with hinterland modernism
yourm large and conspicuous monument
when monuments are refrains
and then she might come closer

in a refrain youm find yourm love, enter
his avenue of arias, his art
aged as yourm own, his notice, needing
then depart to perform yourm nest (while he stays for the rest)
a loose bowl
of sticks high in a branch or a bush, here
cognition begins, transcendent with bricolage

while he invites the spirit with a line
from the firmament
to his short, thick bill, yellow-viridian tint
towards the tip, this
sedentary art engulfed by an insect tide
youm keep re-building until devoured by cat

budgiqwark, wraat wrraat, squealeeyo chew-chewweww!

Moth Orchid

yourm environments & hybrids
moths as orchids, abbreviated
phal for phalaenopsis
Blume (1825), a genus
approximately 60
species, a most popular
hybrid, countless
artificial hybrids, intensive
cross-fertilization, adaptable
to artificial conditions, hybrids
in all hues, all variations
phalaenopsis amabilis
schilleriana, stuartiana
reference the genus phalaena
through India, southern China
Taiwan, Southeast Asia
from the Himalayas to Palawan
Queensland, Zamboanga, Polillo
and the Bismark Archipelago
from East Malaysia to Papuasia, moon bright
resembling moths in flight
a group of large moths, grouped twice
a group of species with a long, branched
inflorescence, with large, nearly round rose
or ghostly tints, a group of species with short stems,
less rounded, waxy with more pronounced
colour, the most common type, epiphytes
some lithophytes, the shattered
colours of rainbows below
moist and humid canopies
through algid, rainless zones, adapted

individually, strong against the light

monopoidal, not
a psuedobulb, not a rhizome, the sudden
intervention of a baroque blossom
a long, spindly stem, one or
two fleshy ellipses
the older, basal leaves drop off
and youm spread into flight
a god emerging in mid-summer
perfect in yourm hour, petals
splayed like a lover in waiting
blood blooming through yourm veins
then stillness, the inflorescence
emerges from the stem, a raceme or
a panicle between yourm ivory fans
glistening, youm listen to the weather,
flower together, pistil
and stamen, pollen, world dew
spoons of vale and water, death
is birth, a call, call, protect
yourm selves with yourm wings

after sex, youm enter senescence
or petals and sepals find new uses
escape death's programme, produce
chloroplasts, fatten and green, photo-
synthesise fucking into theatre
prisms into moist cedar boughs
yourm beauty grows as I turn to die

a beach of fine powder drains
into intricate, bony labellum
yourm tongue reaches beneath
the remnants of a cardinal explosion
long since clustered into signs
and diffuse, lathered wakes,
as though yourm body were a blend
mouth fused to hips, face to sex
swollen pad for the landing, those ruby-
pink rivulets where desire surfaces, scribbles
upon the skin its cursive of roots and
nubs within vermillion convergence,
a node so snowed it spills into pearl, a source for feeling—
here youm float, creamy moth, floury egret
suspended bride, stiff
in lace
in waxy pools of candles
planets alight in space
distance scratched with wingbeats
yourm voluptuous pages
rupture the crux
of their population, phenotypically
plastic expressions
of behaviour, multitudes
of meristems, decentralised sensory
systems, where hope

of this soaked crust
yourm gaudy scar, splashed across the islands
of their most elaborate performance
of wings, of what they might hope, in fantasies
upon a centre, upon a gender, the spectre
slimy when wet, with an imperial insistence
and crisper than the rest, almost
what's loved is almost rubbery, thicker

leaving it all in a blurred lagoon
sucking focus from what surrounds youm
carved from the biome
of a ceaseless stasis, an electric face
the rippled rippling ripples
of milk dropped in a honey pool
and wither, the interminable shock
not found, will only fall
on itself, will not deliquesce if
is little else, insists
beyond vision, but hope
towards the swelling pulse
of its cortex, canals sketched
along the contours of a reef
and hints of expansion
by a wobbling circumference
is a gesture, stemmed

King Parrot

the only Australian red head, brilliant

rear, tchallap—seet? seet? lapped

scarlet head, a claret tipped

a tubby cheeked   fine florid chest tips

waves of sooty burgundy foam   gum leaf   a beak of orange smoulyourm iris in a bee-gold ring

yourm long tail with a bice sheen

pin-striped into azure
on fluorescent lime
intense emerald viridian

intensive plumage
sedentary and dispersive
dense riverine wealds
in flopping palms and
from Cooktown to Port Campbell
down the eastern ranges
in rainforests, in pairs and families
youm chuckle in dripping sclerophyll

into sunset wings, tail

dering cherry belly, mossy and back

dawn rap, yourm shrill of companionship but

arise with erratic, spasmodic acuate chorus, conscious

alone spikey whistles, the perched chreip- to the blue-

to the flooded sky, the high peeip-peip, similar

winged, cheeky similar: rimson osella or tail, no whitish bill

crimson osella but no teal cheeks, shoulders

bottomless eye ringing k-teee-tip the loud central teee

not the rimson osella, the clear k-teee-tip more

until free from view

of escape, yourm fly

of pain, its apprehension, and the joy

yourm screeching flight, a verse

a screeched karrark, yourm tail fanning

a harsh, metallic alarm shoots up

when the uman throws compost on the pile

or when the cat moves through the brush

soaring, penetrating

music than squeak

back to yourm emerald cape, yourm solid

flaming cranium, smooth

carmine, ignited for a slow drip of pure red

yourm complete absorption of sheen, save bulb-shouldered

to where youm started
their wishes get things back
catching up to the idea that layers of stratus
rhythms scrapping the arcs and zags
shafts through a bag of sun
and loosed into whistling
butterflying on stunning bone
splash into gloom
a fleeting, spectacular
then roll, tumble into flock
youm wing yourm way into soaring
to greet the indigo twists
from the canopy, a group cry, youm rise at last
in clear morning, blasting
showing yourm bright, emulous confection, away
parading the joys of yourm changes
or rapid chrak-chrak-chraks
yourm variations, yourm charracks
stinging k-weeks, chreeks
and abrupt, clear krasseeks
direct and regular beats
yourm backswept wings, yourm full
in modest flocks
through the trunks in pairs
below the level, weave
of the tops, youm fly
seldom are youm seen above the green
the lines of yourm like turquoise beams, flouro-azure

lime glow in the noon

here youm come descending
indelicately declining, dropping
into silence, yourm bright
glances, turned this way
and that
clambering on ski feet
aware, awake, the intensity of the object
each particular seen
followed
forage for seeds
for fruit
puppy follow babble
shutter cackle, winged ring tuckled
chuckle, lumpy
looney mate, jookey bloom
bouncing wabbler, brightest looker, so eager
eeager craarck palaver, scraaart
hicchuk, chuckcheckchuck
eggs on a bed
of dust at the bottom
of a hollow trunk
bull-breasted, chickle seeoott with yourm

plrow-plrup, mess up

clawing yourm uck, whaddarp all this nibbling, squeez-

nibbling arp, yourm bellied brottle, knife whistle

ing a berry for juice, youm above, drop the scraps, chickle-seeoot

own this locus, owning it good, look

machine, nibble machine

chickle-teeny waddler, waddling the bull waddle, plow-plrup

Red-necked Pademelon

the first beat's an earthy thud
after the fall, when yourm umbra pounds
upon the lawn's drumskin
a thumped alarm, yourm hind
feet smack
slapped with double force
the thoosh-thash-
thoosh through thoo-bush crisp
spluttering, the snoffle of dry kindling

burning   munching needling lawn strokes   of residuum lips   and sod   nibbling snapped, desiccated stems   nimble bounce   through nobbly   noop, pawooo schlibbit   a lean to sticks   schl-

from their verges, hidden
from the forests of eucalypt and rain

is pulled by yourm mouth
onto yourm snout, yourm becoming
balding stump, youm tilt
hoop pines gathered in a spur, yourm tail's
of yourm face, breeding through a year,
by concentration in the grove
and quivering velveteen ears, eyes condensed
melon with trunk-coloured velour
fluff melon, melon tipping on meagre arms

up flocks
and waiting ones, their hunched-
youm diverged from the others, munching
youm, kangaroo, wallaby,
youm are the image of three morphologies:

once sought by Black and White alike
of Port Jackson, yourm meat
corruption of badimaliyan, from the Dharuk
red-necked thetis of the thylogale genus
navigator of notice, lest I come nearer
melon belly, littlest macropod, strange
a fluff tubble with little mitten tooffle
tipped forward for the grass to read
my emptiness, a woolly gourd
of a furry melon enters
the image of an image
when the pounding recedes
ibby schlibbit the deaf diving and dividing the tiniest vial of modulation

in the thickets, youm emerge
to browse lush grass and shrubs
in the cover of darkness, on the margins
of the east, the red-bellies
to the south, the dusky
northern cousins, this
yourm dense scrubland, yourm undergrowth
yourm tunnels through the briars
of swampy country

once shot, now hunted
by ats, ogs and foxes, forced out by
the explosion of abbits across yourm grasses
we clear the trees, push the wallabies
and aroos over yourm boundary
where youm are pursued
by dingos, hawks and pythons

what was spoken expanded
to yourm running edges, yourm broad range,
funnels of wings into branchlets
so that when youm turn toward
the soothing, when it envelops
enfolds, a polished
entry like a pleat in air, there
all the while, patient
to clasp, yourm languid last
sweetens the wait
yourm singular
vantage, supple
scribbler, spectator
of sleep, take care   the indivisible plumage   the mass of flies   hovering in anticipation

of a coming morning

Antarctic Beech

the pattern of distribution feeds
speculation, the genius
of the dissemination, the dates of
the epoch, the theoretical commons
of Gondwana, of one hundred
million years, then rifts of classical
drift, the northofagus dist-
ribution, coppiced and southern,
Patagonia, New Zealand, Australia
New Guinea and New Caledonia
fossilised pollen from the warmth
of Antarctica

moist, archaic Australia, those soused
southern forests sailing into sun
forcing yourm retreat to the east
to the highlands, creeks like veins
struggling back to yourm nucleus
while the rest marched west
with the gums, such copious heat hushed youm
to the periphery, the penetrated ancient
the known raked into clearings
what rests
in yourm protective cone?

Gondwanan
from flame
the frosty table
to the
of Lamington
the cool tempers
yourm finest
at Werrikimbe

you could think sex

the settlement of the

in the cold
from the plains
horizons, whisky
where youm
black thwarts
rotting
to yourm lagoon
the rust drip
and kings, bins
in vanished books
the test of style
of a god's
restricted
closer to loose-
yourm running
dentured to existence

rain-time relict, freed
by the eastern heights
of Barrington Tops, north
plateaus
and Springbrook
with occasional snows
growth
and Mount Banda Banda

and so unravel / but hermetic in the tropics youm / thrive in the memory of prolific chill / yourm moss

clearing cultures / left yourm shrunken eastern fractions / clumped in parks protected / remnants of

of the high, withheld
inside halved
light malting
touch it, yourm peat-
forked tackle
and paused, en route
youm deflect and bridge
where spiders pool
and wrens tumble together
of eel ossein, fossil horror
the rock
wrangled skeleton
freed stagnant
ned relicts of flesh
stands translocated, in-
with distant source

-laden gnarl through the mists / suggests groups of hoary druids / a hi-mystical realism earlier / than

dank, trans-Pacific pasts under siege / by fiery eucalyptus by agricultural flats / youm are swallowed

a bygone name like negrohead buried / under be-
story than any / lord with a ring
and bled reds orange / in spring half-dropped in
by fire recover / slowly from fire in fire / the ancient is destroyed
inconspicuous yellow-beryl / catkins and fruit of

bark's cleaned by light into truncular flow giant rings
exhibits complications exhumed
jollopped glints of olive or sage in epiphytes
by erosion to the paths
stubble, dashed lichen while new
ech scaly evergreen / leaves of dim willow beneath a crown of twelve
mostly moss below the sun, sites from yourm
autumn triangular / with fine teeth thousand years: emanation
of sparse penetrable, lesser boughs home, yourm
four prickly valves / with mini winged nuts of multiple trunks' post-blaze
of relief, branched sets of smell and rings
meditations
of woodthink dispersal to hopes for

aspergent flicker, gridless in yourm

leanings like a nose coppicing, dying

like a slumped

boles

cold with

so, snake, tangle and yourm base

swells into truck, creates

caverns and hollows, collects mulch

for more roots, thus youm disappear
covered
into yourm own protruding angle
and mosses
yourm mound of mulched stage
shoots coppice
of sleepy clasp, mound city
first base, clone
of fern city, web city, sun-
cloned rings
light and lichen city, cathedral
homes and
of radicle, centre of golden
hundreds, critters
coppice: huts of arced morass
fragments, critters and
extended across withdrawing bays
and stems ringed, ripped
spilling yourm limits over stony littoral
continent, yourm new
sinuous, zig-zagged to yourm jeopardy
yourm huge mind
Antarctic recollection

the silver modicums of minutiae, the budding
standards waver while giants bite
over ridings, stubblings from split, tangled
feet, an expression of crossed legs, stripped
of swoon, intellect
of tree, or intent to tree, not
just tree or trees
but meta-tree, lyre-tree
dissections in
or -forest, sculptor or mimic
youm correct origin cut to
of multiples, form's a base
spores seethe tokenly at impending
not a ceiling, orphaned onto slits
moss rinsed in late light and
leaks a healing, primordial spites relit

an ancestral terror of obstruction
ferns drip with instants, the indolent tumult
released into contours, exposure's very seam
the impervious flux of yourm public heart
fallow wrapped around a stance
venerable material timbered as stuff, relict habitat
filled through the parted stand
toughened immanent semi-shade
yourm abyssal collective written into strings
with the root of an older tribe
of land, bridges across cleared
the r o o t done-
country to yourm primeval family
rooting sieves out-
yourm battalions sheltering their own hollowing
wards in a way gone among in-

sufficiently fed with surplus, coppice

after the fourth bud, selection

of thinness as shade
reluctant to saturate with glaring torrent
closed under charged buffers, ratioed
forks whip unspilt leans, the ambivalence
by the redundance of keys, yourm
secret keys of yourm unfurling margins
tumorous lobes or knots, many-souled
meta-skeleton concealed until blunt glades open
as sundry constellations, profiles
pasture, the into glassed encounter
of new shrubs, flat-leaved ferns straggle
hung to dry
up yourm slopes

Albert's Lyrebird

soil swiftly stripped eetle eaten / munching mulch larvae munched / forage
or disappear into metres / the hundreds of metres of resonance
path runner youm pause behind a beech

sleek pod of scratch, for orms / and ails, yourm
there youm go / swallowing stories like
semitones / like raindrops falling in-

a timid, pheasant-sized Prince, an
sized kingdom shot to be eaten
to increase supply / to globe-
yourm homes vandalised, forcing
shy poets of threats / flourished
varied, the harsh / threatening, the
keys jostling / in the loud antiphonal
three and a half thousand strong
states, scattered / and isolated
in Main Range, Tamborine
near Killarney,

a chestnut

the song patches sing ground
at Lamington at Springbrook / swift-footed
a broken fence is
a rhyme's a moral that becomes a
cool / misty bowl, dewed and   a canopy of eucalypts covers an oasis
grubs, marks / flung like   a sodden forest's function
to stillness
a liar made of leaf litter
Albert, a lyre-   and crumbling into ornaments
in pies   of loves long lost, yourm gerund faded
trotting hunters of curios   of lagoons and shrikes, the parks full
youm higher, fabulous   reduced to sites around the auld Surfers' Paradise
in alarm, the many / and   in the gullies, by the rivers, on the slopes and ridges
whipped Eastern mimic,   in drenched sclerophyllic, bulging over the mesic
contact music
through the division of
sites, Mt. Mistake   brownish grey to darker grey or black, the dancer
and Lamington, Mt. Barney   grey ring around yourm eye / the legs and feet are
the continent's anti-bard   lyre, the brighter and the high, a broad / blue-
yourm iris dark brown or black, the bright
black, yourm brown, yourm impervious
dark brown and yourm lyre, yourm bill / is
brownish-grey, slightly brighter, the lyre / yourm
yourm fore-flanks / yourm underwing is a dark
grades / into grey brown on yourm breast, yourm belly
the slightly and the lyre / yourm rufous-brown foreneck
wing, dark wine to rufous brown / slightly brighter on the rump
and throat / the rest of the dark and the folded / the rest, the folded
head's reddish brown, the prominent / rufous-brown on yourm chin
the rectrices / yourm head and neck are mostly grey / below yourm fore-
brown, yourm simple dark- / grey lyrate rectrices, the dark lyre / the mostly,
verts / the rufous-brown of yourm chin throat and foreneck / yourm rufous-
bright / rufous-brown flanks, the bright brown / flanks, vent and undertail co-
bright rufus colour, the grey and the iris / the brighter, more extensively rufous, the
the high, the brighter and the more / the brighter and the bright, the brown / and the
crest bears a symbol / a perfect shape, the high / lyre the bright lyre, the brighter / and
petals, falling / into upturned bottles in yourm brown / yourm impervious eyes a splendid
glows in morning drizzle / an amber taste of honeysuckle, bent / from the shaft to all manner of

a preference for knots of thick foliage / where youm split yo-

a continental joy
fence

patterns of intonation emerge from the ether / youm b-
in the rumble of the sclerophyll / cryptic calls cracked
elusive and tangling into tents / here's yourm habitat

timid, pheasant-sized / not superb, not a ranger / a
lyre-armed, hen-sized in a frou-frou / chinks in a
gobble spoil with gullet jobble / juggle space with

methods are effaced below spectacular shapes / a
silt-puce plumes, six pairs / of long, filmy and l-
a long, broad and webbed pair of lyrates / a lo-
into glitter over yourm head / or the tail is sho-
and webbed sepia feathers have rounded tips
splits into sky

a master art, a sound / unparted by sight, the
an invitation to future, faked / by bowerbird w-
aeon-sent intrigue, softly calling sella can / me-
crosscut / create an utterance, bottled mellow
powered by dingo, flexed hush kinked / with b-
plains mapped with melody, sonority, link cat-
to slim squeaks and trills like a triller / like a rill
drop through odysseys unfractured by seam /
screaming owl and uman, tapping / clicks, hidd-

youm wait for winters, weeks of / territorial and
yourm gronking, a little clicking, pure stillness /
lustrous jewel atop the line / beneath which all song
of convulsion, gulped / bubbled up eedieai and uddy-
youm wait, yourm dancing forest phone, how / the al-
in arrows, flying through foliage then vaporous / dow-
yourm shared will / until she arrives to quench yourm
of rays / shining into another, the arising / the shining sile-
a display of a few / minutes to over an hour, a visual display, y-

urm beak between earth and sky

urble in the scanty shanty
by dawn / shy and
in dim light and wary

timid presence, hen-sized
quiff display youm
a lyre

central pair of long, ribboned and
uxuriant feathers
ng, tilting train, which youm invert
rter, simpler and slightly drooping
but no filaments / yourm beak

fount / of song, of structure
hile youm bowerbird
w bird too, saw
rising clearer
ells and whips, warble gargle,
tle bell with kettle boil, youm switch
mirrored by the rim of a lyric
into grunts and clunks, cranky presidium
en, another shrill shriek of alarm

sequential anthems, to gronk
above the top beak, that still, ebony eye
is swallowed, ballads
unnunoan, youm mime
one's directed, the alone
nward, towards abandon
silence / yourm bleached centre
ce, buoyed by the new
urm stage…

a stage, a vined amphitheatre

flat plane, arrange

scrape the land back to sound's

concealed by trees, youm rake away debris

yourm ground lyrics polished with mimics

in stage light, yourm display site

of hours and days, ridge poems

the canopy and youm descend to poetry

youm sleep up high, until light spears

learned women come to court

those boulders, logs and branches

where the critics come to visit

the several thin vines, or vines

and fallen branches, striped across

the ground or crossed, crossing each other

on the ground or raised just above it

when the critics come youm come

for yourm platform of sticks and twine

where all genres are destroyed, stages

in lawyer cane patches, sources of screens

the fledgling canes with leaf-sheaths

shorn of sharp spines

by yourm impervious, dancing feet

when locale is drawn into fable, walks into verse
floats back to rest on yourm dancing
yourm mating time or out, any order
feet clasp vines, supplement sight, plume shine
youm clasp and fling those vines like ropes, playing
field like a puppet, curtain shimmer
copse drummer, shimmer plumed half-
fabric, fig tapped ratter
tap tap thicket opera, poem plume
in any order, yourm tail's low, phosphorescent
parabola envelops poetics in silvery
shiny under-plumes, a veil of bushy
filaments quivering ribby
in shim, sticked carols in a cloud
of chalk sketch, a picture
is striking, a costume's percussive
flame gleams beacon against silver, ribbons
of median crossed, swept up and out, flame

what's a territory I'm a dawn territory still
too dark for safety yourm call
from the roost the first
intermittent songs of yourm
self the demonstration
of continued occupation
the dawn call of awakening
the weet-
weet-
weet
weet
weet
weet

rattered tatter
the laced tuft, the rhythm vines, ratter-tat-tatter
the ratter-tat-racket, the plume
pressing and releasing vines of rhythm
oscillating sheens and greens
and yourm dancing on a shaking screen
the ground round's ground, yourm ground's round scratches
sweeping with deliberate prancing foot by foot
vegetation, the vines positioned, yourm medians
the whole dome flickering, the spread
mist, the shimmering whole, the octaves
the curtain cascades over yourm crown in a shimmering
of the whole, the whole whole
their peculiar sheen, the symmetry
the delicate tracery of the elegant filamentaries

chills to silver, a voice picture

the motionless eye, the thawing skull
yourm gulped canticle, a jeep jeep jeep jeep
a jool jool jool jop-
jeep, a calm
an intruder, a battle song blossoms
done, so
circle cyclical, sixteen territories in one hundred and twenty cycles
of mimicry, seconds long, mimicry is the making
the making of repetition, a pause
partitions two parts, staccato notes
some kings, some greys or crimsons
selections of pied and satin
then a series of longer, longer notes

weep!
woop

cycle yourm sequences through
that long-drawn eee-ooo
like territories, steal that bower
a minute without pause, porous sounds
a sequence without pause, nearing
that largest component, the mimics and calls
kwaall, now youm hear that meet!
kwaall, youm hear that meet
tappa-lappa-tap-lappa-
the poem blends into June, range into rain patter, lappa-
youm sing range, sink into its rune
kookazella and roburra, the sequential stage
satinations, yellow crimson, satin
tations, honey eater crimson, whipped
part two's imitations, imimi-

of an invisible wing, the signals
rustling after wing beats, feathers
the beats and the rustling, feathers
a smaller wing, the rapid beats
as a voice alights on a sprig
perfect, perfect wing beats and a thump of the feet
bowers and wing beats, rustling notes, the-the the-the
the mimicked tapper, snapper, satin-
short and very high green, the tapping
satin tenors, mostly mimicked
hide reverb, satin bowers, shhh
flapper, paradise rifle
woo-woo-weet! wing
hoohoo-joooll-woo-woo-
musics, satin calls, yourm territory calls
east the yellow, non-
tones, rapid snapping laugh burra
taps, lurid honey, alarm
y-roollyoo non-musics, beak
brittle-bibble-bert, weep
bribble-bert-chee-werp
jow-hoohoo-weet, weet-chuckle-weet
a log runner, satin bowls, howl
a short, high-pitched green, an Australian king
sweee-sweee-sweee, here she
comes, cherrblat cherrblat walkie-
talkie rapid squelch, the vegetation
synchronised systematically with
walkie-talkie doodles, shimmered symmetrically
with chatter, chuff melody, bubbled
R2-D2 electro squelp, boiling static
popping, if the vines
and sticks are dry, a top-tapping, a wild ditty
with an instrument, rippling rhythm sticks
vines and sticks, gronking's explicit
onomatopoiesis, dubbed
short, loud and blurred pitch
through the chipped dawn with low

of sculpture, the nerves of the forest
the dance of being before it erupts
into form, congeals in an hour

(interval)
a typical interruption:
an approach, an intruder?
a failure, a nearby display, a few
tentative calls left wanting
youm launch into full sequence
with frequent pauses, with more territorial
music
or an alarm! a voice-
picture of the local scene, mimicry
of a variety, of a miniature og
then some alarms of yourm own, of others
or danger! youm interpose periods
of ominous silence between a grey
goshawk's whistle, heighten tension
to hawk's pitch
disaster! youm restore alarm
before exploding into the sounds
of extreme distress

frequency energy / gronks rolling through the undergrowth / beneath blossoms of cracking fog / cracof yourm poem

there's no evidence of overall appearance
nothing lasts as evidence
no evidence of lasting pairs
the overall appearance is a pile of debris
an inconspicuous nest
a conspicuous tambourine
a nested lament is building into ethics,
becoming a nest, youm nest beneath the canopy
the darkest nest, the tenebrous forest, where
nothing lasts but evidence
between rocks, on ledges, in clefts
or inconspicuous caves, cliff faces,
in deep, rocky ravines, near the falling
waters or on the only flats, on steep slopes and
creek banks, between the buttresses of fig ficus
at the feet of palms, amongst stumps
amongst packed ferns and shrubs
in tree forks on occasion
occasional reuse, or return to recover
last year's sun

alone youm build the dome
with a side entrance, a composition
of sticks, bark and fronds
pieces of rootlets, palm leaves and moss
a dome lined with moss, fine plant
material and months of feathers
a poem of hours; a home of weeks

rasping, harsh chant, possum grunt
of soft, homeless notes—then
kling gronks and series

Fallen Myrtle Trunk

in the temperate forests, the wet
sclerophyll forests where tempests
moan in yourm leaves, a storm beating
muffled drums at the entrance
to the underworld, the lands
of Gondwana, motherland of Australia,
South America, the hundreds
of years creeping, the moss about youm creeping
the growling thunder, the grim sou'-wester
—by youm all this recedes, falls
like wilting springs

aged into agelessness, less
than age, giant
fullness, monoforest
bulk
of years and patience
hint of snake while touch crumbles
like chocolate flakes, vibration vanishes
in yourm tomb, tombing
yourm slumber rots, beachwards
a giant petrified through exposure

imperceptible scuttle scattered
deeply, cavern hymns at
cave hertz, yourm august
specific music, cylindrical fugue
of dark russet scales, closed subdued pink
to reddish grain, edified with mountain
ash memory, guardian of closed passage
pillar of larger sky, of facts like clouds
their sky ways wending

youm know the lullabies of loneliness
the ways of wind and rain, youm moan
of fire unless the flames come slowly
for yourm return to drowsy droning
the intoning of the wizard priests
the sough of the southern seas
youm're the stage before the sea
the ground's stage, for all sea-yearning

yourm limbed stances form too
gradually for change, beneath such gestures
the stygian flock shelters, shadowed
in yourm underside, that invisible realm
of canal venom and latticed vein

to the light youm present carpet bridge,
seeds of lives held
by yourm unfolding descent, ink-
plumed monarch, ebony laced
with wing, by the mountain rills
down to the parched saplings
on the shore of a receding lake,
youm know too much
of that escarpment beyond, rest
pray, yourm beast prepares for rebirth

while everything frizzes, shifts
brushed and squeeze, sway
youm remain sound-
like, a solid gradient an always
line, travelling
and unravelling through the same place

yourm skin mimics lake ripple
grooved rivulets criss-cross like thickened years
stone currents into softer solids
edging damp, ripples merged with moss
the land's dry, soft with moss
a surface of crawling speckleds, blood legs and
onyx bodies, orange-like
fruiting bodies protruding from
yourm furry, whaled bulk

moss colony, moss-scape, the stick shade
of a seedling wobbles on yourm chest
flecked with sonnet, leaf voltas
their jade rhymes, lost brilliance

then fresh blush, pinked to orange faded
jagged, triangled teeth
and fruits of three stunted
winged nuts, subtle flourish
of lemon-green catkins, now a mouthing
eddy where a bough broke off
airborne spores of wilt lulled by such knots
have settled on yourm lesion

one branch, there, pleads help
by reaching, others
arch hardened spines around gravity's slide
while youm host the epiphytes
while the termites elaborate yourm runnelled intentions
while moss slowly fingers, surrounds
slowly devours these juts of twig
slowly devours its own ground
which youm perform patiently for it

Housefly

musca dom**estica, of the** suborder
cyclorrh**apha, starting** in the cenozoic
the southern Palearctic, particularly
the Middle East, close **and commens**al
with umans, **so common** in uman
habitations**, comigr**ations to worldwide
di**spersal,** one of the world's widest
distributions, the morning's first pest
the evening's first absence
a life of summer wee**ks, or chil**led months
occasional overwinters in **protected**
crannies, in building crevices, **not**
the neatest, youm **frequen**t dumps, garbage heaps and sewers
then miles and miles **of gutte**rs, strings
of muddy creeks, sh**ining rivers**

youm live close to **yourm ori**gins but youm
can journey far for **food**
for ovipositions **walled in by** cliffs, woodland
boles and bar**ren ridges,** where the horizon's lost
in yourm clouds of madness and ragged
stunted trees, the sneer of the bush
and drought's eternal

summer's string section, a teeny kazoo, a

steaks
harvest**ing yourm m**aggots could feed our pets and
our **manure and sh**rink its risky stench, or
could **exploit youm** to fight our filth, to eat
for recycling nutri**ents and their n**atures / we
of decaying **matter and** so youm matter
yourm larvae feed and thrive in **all kinds**

a needle that sinks in**to yourm he**art
sliver of time, but dissatisfaction's
youm accept hunger and cold like yourm
shit speckled across vast surfaces
beneath your**m continuous** salivation, urination,
that vo**id continuall**y recurring
and quenches yourm endless thirst
transfor**med into ho**ney—it provokes
slurp it in, all yourm desire, sizeless
with vomit, sponge up with yourm proboscis
and meat which youm soften
spoiled fish, eggs
and all sorts of moist decay
from wounds and sores, sputum
material, on what's discharged
semi-liquid su**bstance, fe**cal
so yo**um sponge**-feed on liquid or
regardless of **size, youm** cannot bite it

suffocating fear

turbine of reedy tunes
an obscene drone over the bed, seed
speeder, only by my body **do youm**
stop, slinky tickler, close talker
youm stare playfully, **excitedly**
scorn **polyhedrally**? (my clumsy
mass, my wingless arms) **patter**
catter, youm splinter
curves, weaving yourm coal **threads** in and
out of sight, crazy
sketcher of light**ning script**
alph**abetic spurt**s and
fizzes into nil

in the whine of heat we languish
in the plagues of Egypt, youm
swarm about the water **holes**
of our blighted eyes, hyper-
moto**rs, start fast** into vanish
or daintiest little steps, still uncatchable
unless **I melt into ze**n, youm insist
upon conviction, insist
on yourm ruin**, wherein lie**s salvation
its bright quartz, rest through the night
in corners and cellars
sheds and garages, where youm can
hibernate through frigid winters, thaw

anthrax, leprosy and cholera
bacillary dysentery, ophthalmia and salmonellosis
worms, yaws and typhoid fever
least sixty five to umans, parasitic
under suspicion of passing at
of carrying one hundred pathogens,
a pest, a disease courier capable

a slight curve in the media vein
similar: the stable, piercing mouthparts
more slender; a straight media vein
similar: the lesser, somewhat smaller
sharp bend of the media vein
in-flight stability, the characteristically
reduced to pigmy halteres for
with a wing pair, a hind pair
a hairy ebony nib

between claret, compound eyes
women have more room
male eyes meeting in the middle
yourm male, xanthous undersides
irregular markings on yourm sides
abdomen, its midline,
or black, grey or xanthous
stripes along the thorax, sapphire
of an inch, four
nugget, from an eighth to a quarter
puffed dirt, or crinkly-black mini-

when spring arrives

tuberculosis, tularaemia **and poliomy**elitis
youm regurgitate and excrete wherever
youm rest, **transmit** what sickens us with yourm media
of hai**rs, entrance**s, faeces and vomitus

but yourm fabric, the post-mitotic
cells of yourm somatic
tissue, is long-lived
an informative
model
system for cumulative
cellular alterations, if oxidative
mole**cular damage**
is the s**ource of age**

the point's 500 eggs / up to
150 a batch, their alabaster buds **just**
beyond **a millimetre,** deposited
in decay**ing matter, ex**crement,
preferably horse **manure,** grass
clippings or garbage, in high heat
youm hatch seven and **a half hours**
later, but youm might wait two
days when it's brisk

youm feed on the matte**r in which**
youm find yourmselve**s, first, larv**al
molt, **munching o**n the dead
the decaying, shat
life an**d carrion, yourm** wan-
whitis**h millimetres,** thinner at the pinnacle
and **legless, worming,** living's
brief, then **youm stop eating**
yourm maggots crawling to the cool
burrowing into drier soi**l, where youm** pupate

yourm bloody chestnut pupae, ovals

over populations
for sex determination, yourm maternal control
with **several** mechanisms
and store the sperm for **several egg** sets
might mate just on**ce**
ejaculate **within se**conds, within minutes, mothers
regal purple **pubes**cence
the mounting of the **rear**
the jewelled contours of yourm **probosc**is
youm f**rolic am**ong dung heaps
like **lilies am**ong thorns
after **emerging** from the pupal case
mate just days
from yourm birth place
youm might fly for several miles
if youm starved as larva)
fully grown (smaller
with a few more to roam
in weeks, leaving youm
meta**morphosis, fro**m pallid globe to this
complete

an adult emerges, nevermind which
yourm single hole / in all cases
a single wasp emerges from
sneaky larvae, thinnest thieves
parasitic wasps, those
should youm escape assassination by
into tens of grams, from **which youm** emerge
of transformation, filling

Tea Tree

from a distance youm resemble
Amazonian jungle, a vacant plain
stretching away, cloud-bruised
apple-damp and wired
with road trains, sparkling
rivulets through yourm fecund verb
the ocean learns from the eloquence
of yourm verse, that georgic
twine, uninterrupted as the rivers
dimmed with rotting soil, spread
wide amongst low islands
into mosquito country, mudbanks, bees
in dried-out boughs, from the ocean
youm learn to advance in crawling
packs, to proliferate meticulously,
flooding valley after valley
wherever youm stretch, gently
bending with the breeze, curling like
the waves upon the beach, the pestle's
constant pounding, crushing the air
into pixels of light, lulling minds
into a cushioned impulse
which saves them from vacancy

multiplied
Tree Café in Quezon City,
Filipino cafes, the Tea
cute in the Philippines
wide range of habitats
pea, or succulent, yourm
flat Australian matt-

blushing with sonance, when
youm are pricked, shhh and sex, sem-
blance flows and sibilates
a forest froths the juice of a cure
yourm carpet laid across the land's
worn cradle, bolts of charcoal and bone-
dry lightning through yourm woodlands
while the heavens writhe with lime fire,
blasted pink pockets clocked
with whisker clusters
a flower of clubs, which starts
to spin like a wheel as I watch it
into dream gestalt, Australia's errant marrow
gone and sprawled across the north, fickle

yourm fibrous
flaky bark's the paper
on which logic rests
in the shade of small, rigid leaves
and their crushed aroma
over archipelagos while the hepialid moth's larva
Malaysia, Sumatra, Borneo
javanicum, amboinense
a journey down the Queensland coast
on moist, low nutrient loam
towards the southern scoparium flourish

from yourm ovary's vague depression;
so that a single style arises
within a crimp, atop a fringe
the flurried multiplication along a stem
what youm ask becomes specific, circumspect
in alternation with the petals
five groups of stamens
petals of cream and vermillion, their bracteoles and sepals
rays, flaring yourm five conspicuous
a cut fuzzy for stutter sheen with slashed
crossed and a glimmer

can revere the town of yourm heart
who, in the silence of yourm thought
true dignity abides in youm
true science leads to love
burrows into yourm being:

the compassion of yourm intention
youm speak what youm see, curious bowls
of what the earth says
which waver slightly with the weight
all travel derived from yourm questions
the shock of the terrain, its directions
from this comes yourm law:
the lines of the southern lands
before arcing into cobalt to chant
from which they depart, tenderly
for which all the poets search
winged codes for each tiny, sacred pool
a poem with myriad first lines, five-
within its question huddles a ring
of slender doubts
bowed over a citron tarn
and awaiting yourm utterance
or a visitor's touch, into whom youm
will release yourm writhing menagerie,
excretion into the hum
of her inclination, to launch
for the trails of the sun, sweet nectar
harvest, an archipelago's hesitations
are yourm edible map

tea in the leptospermum genus
shorter members of the myrtacae
a myrtle family of eighty-six trees
the settlers who boiled yourm tasty leaves
an Australasian family, bulked,
like the word, upon the continent, or scattered
worldly in cultivars, in bonsai binds
which are all prone to scale
and subsequent black smut

split at the tip for deliverance
yourm fruit's a woody capsule

Spinifex Termite Mound

from the north the fierce gale blows / a lighthouse of a dwelling encircles its dialects

we are those who ramble about / the upturned caves and shrink / beside yourm stalactites when they projecting what persists into plots / sentinels at a coast those signs / of stern purpose of terra popu-

jag / through from yourm furious cities

with a single swoop the hoe / removes the top of one and then

yourm processions beside the melting bitumen
dried, withered up and ossified,
like giant prickly pears
yourm malleable impositions
hexagonal, blobbed unfoldings
to birth, hived
long smashed, yourm shrines
petrified mustards from jars
appraised by emergency and apostrophes
aging into the shadows of afternoon,
lous their warnings

dismantles the rest pulling walls / off a dolls' house yourm sudden / swarm within exposure a dense

through a syrup of languid ozone
breathable only with speed,
fire walkers, yourm feet bubbling
where youm stop, among the boulders
of peaks youm shall ever sit

translations of grass of bristled / fields milky with late light / into staunch choir salivated on

chunk dislodged / a squashed soccer ball which cracks / open to reveal yourm noqueen on a saucer

youm shall ever sit, this
by limb, a band of sisters
yielding limb
now arable in their endings and mean
from scalding corners
of grasslands, buoyed
in sparse bars
to rise, to draw stillness
built to fill bars of scrub with time,
and onwards the idea of a yawn / welled into scenes yourm bold chords

further in, series / of ballooned chambers connected to branching passages / to absorb changes

may not be
a structure, this may
be a fungus, the east
wind's blowing fiercely, Gaudi's
cathedralesque, spires of drooping
lumps, flaming shocks in the half-
lit thousands, millions of gullets
stuffed with chopped grasses, crossed
axes curling into thumbs
resting beneath index fingers,
all giving way to, built around
a tree's venerable cylinder, a restless
rib drawn into sun catcher
sky sculpture
foom fort, hoom dam, how
the webs ascend into halved-
horse design, doored
mortar, a heaped creature
sprawled around a trunk, piled up beside it
globbing and glugged up

this obese
while youm clean
in the arms of a coterie to
to grub size and her eggs stream
her sweating corpus is swollen

below

in pressure channel the flurries / through yourm apperception this / extraordinary organ not chimney

eggs for years
of polis, hundreds of millions of
organismic epitome, a captive ovary, source
slave, super-
and youm feed her
yourm nurseries
away

her pit sits yourm largest organ / a symbiotic garden / production of yourm long tunnelled exits to

spires / no residences stacked in high rise / but lungs breathing / through yourm porous walls a subwith bandicoots youm're beckoned / with furry tailtips on the precipice

digested mixtures of bushy slaw, such
cellulose into potent, partially-
which sprout and dissolve tough
which youm seed with fungus spores
of fungus combs
youm defecate, assemble into mazes
faeces, chewed grass and lumber, which here
to pack intestines with pseudo
forage

fungus is the becoming
of yourm external stomach, so much
is done for fungus
that fungus gets the better deal
ensconced and constantly tended
recipient of all yourm benefits:
food, shelter, water, protection

great is the

terranean city arises / with gaseous regulation

yourm are forever remodelling / what made the models

tear drops chasing each other searing yourm
parched cerebrum, the fungus collective filling
yourm metabolism, how it signals, controls,
how its chemicals compose yourm spire,
staring at the foothills unflinchingly,
watching the hoarse cries of the hawks
settle on the ground

a faint rustling from / within the volumes

in charge of the relationship?
blue, who's
their exertion in the widest
by the haziest bells, intoning
crowded, fellowed loops, hitched
builders, eager architects,
little sensed of pain or toil, brave
and mass on a smell-plan
towers that scatter
love that hides within youm gluing

yourm / pack expectancy stretchy multiplicities swarming / strata exploded by rupture to cool / to gr-

and dirt flows towards the problem
and as youm surge youm grow
with dirt and surge toward the source
yourm masses fill their maws
and to vibrate / roused,
youm run, news-filled, to nudge
disturbance its sign,
of gases at the first
in humidity in concentrations
air movements to shifts
to novelty alert to slight
or youm rest in collectives, massaging ear sticks, attuned
journey, a restless urge to move
army shuffling and ever-curious, an endless
a nervous suspiration, yourm vast

izzled travel that slips imperceptibly / into the earth thinking's packed / into slabs elastic as any geolo-

and soon the hole is plugged

to have said that youm were once in be-

gy / essence is complexity

tween / and yourm ability to notate tongues / the only way to praise the lay / of depopulated country yourm layered billions alive / in wads of marly lace recycling / ecology and restoring it to sky / every

from spurs and ridges youm weep
in this city of clay lingam altars
immense coal vines fuelling into monsoon
and meta-cobras fireworking the bush
anthem without repose, cobras
as the day turns cinematic and hours
bonanza for iders, ogs and izards, youm sustain this flume
stricken but to whom, a food
currency one becomes in being
yourm hordes of alates
simultaneously from many colonies
flight's a generation burst

driven into the hidden the road / trains and eroded middens / the toasted swamp of a heavy heart

risen to melt, while the
which youm twist into frozen creatures
and absorbed in nodes
inches into monoliths, meads are mown
shards bricked into inches
yourm monuments are planned, moments nibbled,
here in the rubble, in the sand
brain-burnt beyond lures
where yourm stumps regather, outlast

in the harsh tropic spin
yourm abundance, yourm luxuries
through yourm underground activity
feed yourm machine, thread moisture
youm thrive with year-round humidity,
struggle in such aridity
decompositions—the bacteria, the fungi—
through the dry? its common
what can sustain this cycle

is most precious re-enters the soil
when yourm nests decompose, what
the shat and spat matter of yourm walls,
housed inside youm it soars, or stored in
season clutter awaiting mild inferno,
from cellulose, from dry-
aerial injections of food into systems, liberations
dried cities of flying worms
estuaries of undergrounds
and dozing fridges
on roads, beside the hunched pub, its boab
of throng calculus, youm erupt on verges
spirit-filled, weathered inscriptions
monuments to immortality in a Godless country,
yourm buttressed cathedrals of the spinifex
the savannah carved out by yourm intellect
the gravel hills, the remnant towns
bluffs rise with parallel reasons, fire culture's conquest of timber country:
from the depths they ascend
thick stands of mountain grasses in their wake

in the vault of the sky they scream
as they come swooping down
and mountain hawks scream for youm
and sprawled across multiple blocks
to skyscrapers high as a mile
mount into meters, equivalent
of a cauterised continent, cathedrals
youm strike through the smoke
so across the tropical savannahs
can't be sustained
where suitable microclimates
until yourm temperate limits
everywhere a spirit stopped, stops has its marker
like yourm leaf-cutting cousins anchored under yourm Dreaming-turds,
youm cut trails between yourm castles ancestors of the Dividing Range
expand surface for ventilation
of grassy storage, systems to suit
local conditions, yourm humid variations,
with a trunk, foliage and plant-
like roots, stuck until youm move

pins of yourm music
where the ordinary's riddled by cylinder
mile after mile of freckled shade
a wake of low-cool pressure through
slicing up from yourm leading edge
and a kestrel sheds the sun from a wing,
as they come swooping down

Hamersley

arid and tropical, tropical
semi-arid, cycles of
summer cyclones, thunder
at forty degrees, then heaps
of frosty winter nets

the inland uplands of the Pilbara Craton
the Hamersley Range, the Chichester Range
Earth's oldest surface, yourm fossilised
purpose, stromatolites and granites
and three billion years glittering
at Strelley Pool, the cell morphology
of mineralised globes of bygone
beech, dancing moths and
timber bound in crystals, littered
through eroded gorges, Bee and
Wittenoom Gorge, Kalamina, Yampire
and Dales Gorges with
Brockman iron, Wittenoom dolomite
Mount McRae shale, continuous erosion
of summit idiom, of waxen stem
and radix cant, hefty
vocabularies of wind wear, odes
becoming storm, the descent
into stone, into gorges marked
by waterfalls and water holes

the immediacy of Indjibandi, all-present
convergence
the dots
pots

snake scrawl, snakes at city length
vegetation fizzling into mound
into mount, snakes
scrawling in from far off, one
after another, salt and city stained, lyric
was like this, a snake
and her children, HUSSHH, she said
and listen to the valley gushing seared pine
a billowing scud of leaf and wiry lumber
the top of an outlook, the prick of a place
the poem blooms into cool slope

the ancient, tropical trick of the
granite fists,
in this pairi-
to sand-beat,

the turbulent, trembling ancestry
of baked surf, forested spur
across the first ocean, the scrub
flocks around scars, frolics
in molten, magnetic words
which birds hurl in arcane phrases
one million scars in parallel
a phantom's long nails clawing for traction
if I had long nails, my clawing for traction
for map vernacular, expressions
jammed into shapes, canteens
of dust and wonder filtered
through a daze, we suck the drawl
through wilted straws, while
petroglyphs bubble in the blood
the bells of the continents chime
the last poet withers into egg
as the sun's ripped from the sky's chest
and the moon rolls down the back of the night
now the bone land opens its eyes
and slowly rises to the stars

of point and extension
of the chronicles, dotted
dispersed impulsion
through the olive python, euros
and geckos in yourm fragile
acacia and spinifex systems
legless lizards remembering lore
stygofauna in aquifer frore
Marandoo, Brockman
Channar, West Angelas and
Paraburdoo inhaling ore
the mulga parrots and echidnas buzz
and nuzzle, disperse their intentions

mode, whether
dolerite fists, my hopeful wheezing
ng I'll rest
salt-plain span, take me back

vertebrae arc to breach the surface
the terrain's deep night, these layers
of terrors, delirious marriages
of rainbows and comets
yourm tomb cracks in the well of the sea
all breath catches
and vertigo dangles, swells the temples
ruptures what veins are left

stitches simmer at noon, yourm wound
rips open to reveal a mine
and a bold geologist
with her zephyr cape counting
the footprints of goannas in space
she's humming to herself
on glissading, magical tracks
to have the groove of the poem
go back to loam

the Pilbara, region of pindan
shine, star-glossed, rings of grafted
quanta murmur around gravity's
tough rivets, the mirage
lifts the cliffs into undulating country
of buckled summits, sparkles of tentacle
thrash from a crispy lake, who is that
beneath this body?

burial of rhyme in lake plume

youm turn all ascents towards youm
turn light towards youm then
bury it, lengthen into music
as I fly overhead, yourm flashing channels
yourm enchanted chords, what I see
is but part of what youm have been
today I see youm faintly, thinly
veiled in a silky westerly, accelerating over the stony esc-

protrusions of fragment / flesh
needn't have existed
cacophonies of ore and silicates
I'm flying out, I'm breathless
but all moving shadows must fall
a word walks into hilly country
and burns up beside a beautiful gully
something long is waving effortlessly
the distance from my lungs to the land
the eddies of reflections whirling wider
I'm flying out, I'm breathless
I'm a fossil of Altazor, what will catch me?

and brainscape, rucked
crust consciousness

arpments
set free, singing a sphere
and a portion of its rotation
singing a •

0 0 0 0

Lake Mungo

the evidence of habitation's endless: preserved / in a treasurehouse, plundered, awaiting plunder / to

yourm stories in the tucks
fireplaces, burials, spear tips and middens
grasses and seeds ground to flour, knives
for butchering fish, mussels, many small
mammals (bandicoots, wallabies
rats and rat kangaroos)
scrapers carved wood, cleaned skins
hatchets filed to an edge to strip
bark / axes, spears
flat stones, knives: bridges between
thing and things; origins veiled
in a land of sand and clay
the vital value of silica, often
traded from far away, hard and fine-grained
with smooth fractures, hatchets
from hundreds of kilometres to the south
yourm silcrete skeleton, fossil soil
cemented with silica as the water leeches,
layered into outcrops across yourm lakebeds
quarried by yourm people

one day
a group of men chased a wallaby
across yourm muddy claypan while a group
of women walked across youm too
and a child wandered, as children do
then youm dried out, baked their
tracks hard in clear, parched air
to be buried in the drift, the world's
longest path to the Ice Age winding

he
keeping
hunting big
he lives on yourm
Aboriginal man, Mungo man
of abundance drawing to a close
man, forty two thousand years ago, the time
Mungo man, the continent's oldest

towards a dream, where a woman / holds fire in a nugget of termite rock / lets it out at

rock the record with the footprints / of twenty thousand years, two thousand / generations of Willan-
drans, their tools,
grinders, axe heads
going back further, reaching back, thriving
amongst yourm lakes, adapting to the dry
hunger of the Ice Age, survival
of presence, yourm rusty contemporary
of topography:

there he sat on chilly
or turn his palm
he could no longer extend his arm
of bone broken off,
worn from throwing the woomera, bits
in the winter cold, his right elbow was so
with age he ached with arthritis
of water reeds to make twine,
from gritty food, from stripping the long leaves
his molars scratched and worn
he grew tall

out his lower canines when he's young
his rituals keep youm strong, knock
traces yourm origins with his footsteps
men's knowledge safe
game, caring for Country
shores with his family

the next stop the whole / ground to fidget finger and / swoon across the place of yourm places

evaporated
and his ancestors
which had nourished him
then yourm lake
to become the world's oldest such ritual
and sprinkled him with ruby ochre
on his back with his hands interlocked
buried him in yourm lunette
his family mourned, carefully
hunting life, and died at fifty
he reached a good age, for a hard
nights beside the fire / gently rubbing yourm ancient joint
forty thousand years ago
along yourm curve of shattered satellite
where human hours unravel
Mungo Lady's living by yourm beach
yourm basins full and teeming
yesterday's blown from her face
Mungo Lady, mother of mothers
daughter of mothers
the generations of Mungo until yourm Dreaming
she collects tucker, wattle seeds and fish
yabbies, emu eggs and shell fish
nourishes her culture and teaches
her daughters women's lore

when she died her family mourned
youm ghosted her in ochre and
they cremated her, pulverised her bones, burned
them again and buried her
by yourm milky singing lake

the shock of Lady Mungo

and rested; no volcano pierced yourm crust
with subtle but decisive movements
youm rose from the brine
bound by this venerable, stable continent
yourm unique qualities are without accident

yourm hymn of perpetual death unwinding
laid back to rest in yourm lunette
until she was recovered
for twenty years she cried
shelf / her people heard her cries
broken into a suitcase for a university
jigsaw of history and Country
yourm always story, the five hundred-piece
of the sacred in her hands / she already knew
and begins to re-surface with the basis
hears Dr Bowler trampling
she hears the scientists trampling
with her script of human spirit:

and spilled its violent heart; no glaciers
gouged through form; the dunes
that arrived from the west failed
to swamp yourm lakes / youm waited
for the deposits of water and zephyrs,
erosion wearing down the distance
while elsewheres washed across the plains
and along Willandra's ancestral track, sentiments
dumped in the still drink of yourm basin
this sediment of sentiments, matter
of what matters blown from yourm bed
by the westerlies to build
year by year, layer by layer, the crescents
around yourm eastern perimeter, yourm special
archive, storehouse of highlands
washed away, records
like the pages of a book
burying the beginning ever deeper

subtle scape, precious window
into Australian acumen, the stories
of climate and soil are stored inside youm
their genres of dunefields, dehydrated

we come to yourm futures at last
to share their crafts with the living
souls of the dead country come

along yourm walls
with vegetation, voracious stalwarts
a dry, windy lake, rimmed
with alkaline archives
dropped and youm became a salt lake
then came the ice, the water
with smoke from far-flung campfires
children in yourm shallows and a sky laced
umans hunting, gathering food
giant aroos on yourm foreshore
izards and andicoots, ombats and
of water fowl in yourm shoals
when youm brimmed with fish and yabbies and flocks
before the last age of ice
with water from the Dividing Range
written in lower rainfall and frigid nights
the richness of yourm Mungo layer
rivers and distant sierras

youm reveal pockets of yourm past
freely, millennia
eroding from the socket
of yourm giant eye, the old
reddish layer of Gol Gol
buried far below
then Mungo's steel-grey, from fifty
to twenty-five thousand years ago
blanketed under the tanned sands of yourm
Zanci, all creeping eastward: youm reveal
history's carcass as youm progress
youm reveal what descends
until futures unleash reversions
a Man and a Lady convene worlds, having been dispersed in them
they are returning, they will return

the subtlety of Aboriginal time / the force of White settlement
in yourm lakebeds, dunes and sediments
yourm plants and animals, their evidence
stories in the land as we see it

a kangaroo skull on the Mungo lunette
a reimagined giant wombat tends
to disappoint

a scatter of waste flakes
with a corestone

a quartzite core exposed
on an eroding surface

typical knapped artefacts

coming together, Garnpung, Arumpo and Banoon
coming together, Mulurulu, Baymore and Pan Ban
of the moon, the language of Willandra
within the bellow of a raindrop / across the wafer

for heat traps
of capped termite nests, broken up
of baked clay lumps; the shiny plates
emaciated charcoal limits; a bed
that we see:
beneath the same stars
from the Ice Age, where they cooked
of human experience, antique hearths
like the feelings of yourm fireplaces, nodes
were cooked with force
excursions into the moments when rules
yourm magnetic alignments, geomantic
clay hearths preserve

the Lachlan and the Murrumbidgee
through the Darling, the Murray
mammals and freshwater mussels strung
of golden perch, trout cod and yabby
middens of many, many meals, accumulations

strewn across yourm scape
then broken or blunted
of throwaway knives, razors tapered
a scatter indicates a campsite / flakes
flakes and cores from knapping
and axes; waste
the rest are uman argument: grindstones
for blanched nodules of calcium carbonate
but scarce around yourm lakes, save
the facts of stone, most durable of matters

all the way to Prungle, too, youm are
coming together, sliding towards
a wall of stained china, uncovering
revelation, its scarred magnets, ultimately,
no matter its repetition, any single object—
/ (gnarled trunks lopped into fence posts)
(a road's orange smear through a beryl mat) \
\ (the skeleton of a woman, of a man)
must recede, squashed into its undoing as it compacts
into wall, that slightest sierra, sign of yourm purest
force, bending beneath the frayed fact
of the universe, its slippery cerulean lid
compressing immensity until it fractures
into fissured script
termite towers shot from the terra cotta
pebbling, runnelling, the running bodies
become licks of cool fire

spirit and place, three tribes come together
Mungo: meeting place
yourm knowledge is shared, yourm uman statements
yourm children grow strong
in the footsteps of their ancestors

ancient teachers return
ancient proof of endurance, of survival
special Man, special Lady
to be laid to rest in one's own Country
the precious gifts of ancestors, of story
Mutthi Mutthi and Nyiampaa
the people of Willandra, Barkindji,

yourm lake spirals into sacred
into gold letters on swarthy swirls, pale
spirals of ceremony, the paths
of umans which have come and gone
yourm golden richness, strong
strong people
gently carve yourm symbolic tracks
and spray creamy walls
with powerful shade, blood, yellow
and ochres say youm live here
yourm Murray, Darling, Mungo bones, teeth
beneath the Nullarbor, caves, the desert
shares beliefs, sawfish, western sharks, stingrays
lyres in a freshwater gorge

the Ngyiampaa give welcome from the north:
yammah guddah   yammah guddah
ngallia ngurrampaa
welcome to our Country

the Mutthi Mutthi give welcome from the south:
telki thangurra   pirnmatha
welcome to our Country

the Paakantji / Barkindji give welcome from the west:
paliira kiirinana   parimba
our Country is beautiful   please come

yourm drained location, unique / position in the centre of the Basin / to the west
the mallee / then the dunefields of the desert / to the east, a riverine
plain to the Dividing Range / in between, nineteen lakes strung
together / like a necklace of desiccated / dams along yourm
creaky lineament

a low, subdued landscape / yourm walls' humble
scales / their lexical circles, rims, shells / of
hollows where the wind passes, plays / the
reedy shrubs, what's within? / vast sagacity
of secluded meaning, signs of tumultuous
times, yourm lumpen / expanse splot-
ched with ochre / chalky rivulets
and overwhelming / settlements
of olive-teal / big skies vacant
spaces and earthen calls / endur-
ance reaching beyond the horizon
to times long gone, with us still

what we see, what youm show:
millions of years of complex / for-
ces, millennia of human witness
merest snapshot of modernism / the
sheep and the emus scattered over
yourm black / algal cake, where earth
tanks bank yourm water / going back
further, large scalds and claypans were work-
shops, campsites / through calcium and lime-
stone nodules youm blossom into pearl / amidst
the poison of the ripped warrens / the bloody stains
of iron oxide in the continental dunes / histories
connected with Country / living land of the basin's mallee
plains / interminably moulded by wind and rain

Mungo, Leaghur / and Garnpang dominate, stale playas with / mosaicked beds of
grey and heavy red clays / channels and gilgais where yourm imperfect softness / absorbs footsteps in

up from the termite caverns, fume, fools, flexure
which speaks in objects brought up,
recede now by yourm silent wall
bluebush mobs and their crisp scrawl
who heard the scurry of children's feet?
who is the man who's calling?
youm sprawl then muster then run from sight
there's a version, there's another
the secret voids as a spear's let loose
cats and emus draft the directives
what they recall, what youm recollect
the vertical vanishes into movement
egg of clocks splitting with aridity,
to flour, fish to net, fibrous
the changing walls of the moon, seeds
of lives becoming sandrush
beyond the lunette, floods
east into Country—
flees into dunes that balloon and surge
stranded in pillars, while yourm sand
spectacular argil sentinels, stripped
creates yourm rills and residuals
what's soft or muddy washes away
locked in the bones of yourm megafauna
the marrow of the universe remains
the colossal evidence of the upper three
of Golgol, Mungo, Arumpo and Zanci
the pastoral stations, the hearths and middens
the different eras, different climates
the four major layers of the Mungo
gullies of the Walls of China
cloaks of vegetation, the eroded
the stable Leaghur and Garnpang beneath their
whites and consolidated clays
by the chests of the lunettes, their loose
silence—

with sudden crick of mandible, molar
yourm horny skull catches the gusts
translates them into fossils—not the language
of words (their hazy dice hunting for weight) but
poems of backwards, anchored in things'
fuel of forthcomings, pasty
inflated fingers grasping
for yourn laggard, eastward travel
yourm eternal insistence, which gathers weather
watery plenitudes
or their buried talismans
yourm dunes and their variations: parallel swales
of calcareous, loamy scarlets; swales
of deep, sandy parabolas; tall, unstable
dunes of sugar white interspersed
with loamy umber flats, while
the sandplains undulate
with calcareous
vermillion, with
the occasional grey depression

from where it begins
bottled in the copperburrs, the Belah
woodland framed by firetrails, the fish
and the waterbirds are long gone
myriad small mammals are missing
but fauna remains central to yourm mystique
the galahs and blue bonnets
after plain after plain of black bluebush
terrain eroding with warrens or packed
up in hard termite rock
glimmers of red ringnecks
white cypress erupting from yourm bluffs
or death withheld in the desert's broombrush
all recedes before yourm shores
swooping down over the bluebush
on and on until the lunettes of the Wall arise

'

proffered or what they can
and artists of the air descend to kill what's
except the size of sight, which balloons
in just a few minutes the aggregate's miniscule
is watching? who is stepping from what?
with those blonde clots of fruit, who
the idea plummets into a plane pocked
a good area to view, a good area for grazing
the twisted summer lignotubers, mallee of the dunes
there, snaking through the underground
the western greys, while there, there and
or wallow beneath the pines with the reds and
they hover on the banks, imagining rain
the geology magicians rise to read them

to write their stories in the night—
whole varieties of birds, of invertebrates
the abbits, oxes and oats
leaving the roos, emus and dunnarts
strangled from yourm salty clay
what's left of the path? all timber

yourm squat, endless line marbled / with cloud shadow but towering over thought / while small, lime

yourm plant communities
distribute across conditions
of drainage, of salinity / mixed
shrublands: needlewoods, tussock
grasslands in the wet
areas of yourm lake bed
the lunar communities: mallee
cypress pine and sandhill wattle
butterbush and rosewood, black
bluebush and needlewood

along the western edges of yourm lakebeds
white cypress pines on yourm deep
red country, their rot-
resistant resins, once so popular
for fence posts, shed stumps, pink ockatoos feast
on seeds from baby cones,
mature pine communities along the Foreshore Walk
tawny undulations of timberland across yourm sandplains
the herb and grass stories
the densely warted cones of the blue-green mallee
the larger cones of the olive-green Murray
the scaly foliage of the blue-grey-green white cypress

isolated gangs of acacias
in heavier soils, the dominant mulgas
the yarran, nelia, the native and exotic herbs
and grasses

globes glint in the early / light, incessant ends to yourm silent sentences…

youm stop to wait for the tens
of reptile races,

open mallee shrublands, the fruit
of white mallee eucalyptus
mallee shrublands on yourm interdune plains
mixtures of mallee eucalyptus, the yorrell
the white mallee, red mallee, understories
of narrow-leaved hopbush, Aboriginal
mallees: multi-stemmed trees, the woody
structure of the lignotuber, communions
on yourm sandy ridges
of shallow sands and sandy clays, a variety
of mallees on the Mallee Walk and the Mungo Track

a nobbi
unbanded delma, a three lined
knob-tail, yourm largest, the harmless
carpet python, metres and
models of patience, hanging from the branches
in wait, packing up camp when luckless
superb coffee with coal splotches
and yellow arrangements, a creamy
wave through the scrub, or a yellow-
faced whip snake, a bearded
dragon, a king brown / the dangers
of the king brown/mulga,
of yourm eastern and western browns,
but a shingleback/stumpy tail/sleepy
izard rests under scrub with an
earless dragon, its buff
raven and orange outfit lined
with thin frosted stripes, and central
bearded dragons sun themselves
in unusual but practical places
or Gould's goanna, a mallee dragon
a threatened western blue-tongue
a threatened spinifex blue-
tongue and ogs, hidden amphibians, a common
spade foot oad, a long
thumbed og, spotted
grass frogs around the water tanks
the threatened painted burrowing frog

the extinctions of the small since the Whites
following smells, electric scents

digging into nests and mounds
yourm logs and stumps

or a short-beaked echidna ripping open
or the western pygmy possum

must not be eaten
of the eastern grey, which

through the scrub, and the blackless grey
with rust, scattered

the western grey scrubber, sooty grey tinged
with the rain, unlike

from earth he approaches bluebush, roams
in woodland shade

or resting in a scratched-out pad
in that morning light, grazing quietly in yourm grasslands

a red aroo scratches himself

while yourm carnivores persist:
fat in the tail of the fat-tailed dunnart
the common dunnart, nocturnal trails
upon yourm dunes or the southern ningaui, this tiny
energy, eaten out by oxes and ats by grazing
by hot blazes and habitat loss, but microbats
litter the sky, roost
in hollowed trees in old farm buildings

pairs of ringnecks in the mallee community / screeching flocks of galahs across the dome / galahs at

some birds legs grow long / as rodeos, prance through the bluebush / while the pink ockatoo finds

a wedge-tailed eagle feeds on rabbit / a common bronzewing in her nest / flocks of sociable apostle-

on a stump to savour yourm reward
clutched in talons she alights
a mouse, an invertebrate / prey
tucks her wings / dives for
for yourm signs
kestrel, tan-coloured wonder watching
a hovering sparrow hawk/nankeen

everything stops with a butcher's flute
vivid cherry bonnets and aprons
cream belly and mottled sanguine tinges
scans the fringes of yourm mallee habitat
while the brilliant crimson chat
an orange chat runs through the saltbush
a rare Australian bustard
Australasian pipits, variegated fairy wrens
eaters, bronzewings
igeons, singing honey-
budgerigars, zebra finches, crested
rumped arrots, blue bonnets
pink ockatoos, red-
prattle and jabber around yourm tanks:
rest in tree hollows during a drought we all come in for a drink

refuge / hundreds flocking in to roost / ockatoos screeching at sunset, emus / on the lakebed

birds / scrounge about yourm camps, bludger birds / rummaging for scraps

threatened species
persist: pink
ockatoos and mallee fowl
the bustard and the whistler, chestnut
quail thrush

youm don't look
like eighteen thirty
with whiteness came abbits, feral
oats and heep
I destroyed yourm vegetation, increased yourm erosion
exposed more of yourm primordial remains

the pressure builds
all the aroos come running
through yourm undergrowth
on the back of a sheep
on the sprays
the cow's nutritious favourite
the old man
so many weeds
of overgrazing
so many lives
the logged acres of cypress
struggling
of the abbits
threatened belah
acacia scrublands in decline:
and
even sadder
macropods have thrived
water supplies

like the water in yourm dams
and extinctions crepitate
Australia never rode
we rested
of old man saltbush
these days
is hard to find
have invaded in the wake
crowded yourm thoughts
are in decline
pine, their seedlings
midst the jaws
oats and heep
and rosewood
mulga, nelia
yarran / the story's
for fauna / the larger
with dammed
but eighteen are endangered / and so many others are gone the litany / of names of those I haven't

the ~~bridled nailtail~~ wallaby

the ~~eastern hare~~-wallaby

named:

the ~~brush-tailed~~ and ~~burrowing~~ bettongs

the ~~northern hairy-nosed~~ wombat

the ~~western barred~~ bandicoot

the ~~bilby~~, the ~~numbat~~

Notes

The poems in *Lyre* draw on a variety of sources, including relevant literature from plant biology, ecology, geography, geology and zoology, my own field notes, and poetry from different languages. Fragments from these sources were combined into collages and incorporated in the early drafts of each poem. Subsequent revisions modified these fragments substantially, but traces of the source texts remain. In particular, I wish to acknowledge that *Lyre* contains echoes of the following:

Nephology
'The Macaw', by Sarah Holland-Batt
'is it is', by Peter Minter

Oceanic Manta Ray
'the shadow's keep', by John Anderson
'Manta Rays and Humpbacks', by Wapirrku Kanturrpamarra (trans. Alexander Brown & Brian Geytenbeek)
'Rays', by Rose Lucas
'Poem Written after September 11, 2001' & 'Poem Written from November 30, 2002, to March 27, 2003', by Juliana Spahr

Whaleshark
Apocrypha, by Peter Boyle
'The K' & 'Merce of Egypt', by Charles Olson

Pacific Green Turtle
'The shadow's keep', by John Anderson
'After Hermann Hesse's Wandering' & 'Still lifes (iii)', by Dan Disney
'Ecuatorial', by Vicente Huidobro (my trans.)

Western Clownfish
'Resolution', by W. S. Merwin
'Clownfish', by Stan Petrovich
'Ancient History' (trans. Clare Cavanagh), 'Albi' (trans. Cavanagh) & 'Moses' (trans. Renata Gorczynski, Benjamin Ivry & C. K. Williams), by Adam Zagajewski

Shallow Estuary
'Estuary Sonnet', by Alice Oswald
'Estuary Bed', by The Triffids

Mangroves
'Salamander', by Octavio Paz (trans. Denise Levertov)
'Mangroves', by John Watson

Sand-bubbler Crab
'think of this', by Christopher Kelen
'Asemia', by Angela Rawlings

Fireflies
'the shadow's keep', by John Anderson
'Ixtlan, on First Visit' & 'A Time for Body Prayer', by Marjorie Evasco
'Four Lines', 'Vanitas', 'Eros Diptych', 'Study of Linearity', 'To Have Witnessed' & 'Study of Linearity (Denver–Manila, 2006)', by Marc Gaba

Gecko
'Recuerdo', by Maria Luisa Aguilar Cariño
'(In)Visible', by Michelle Cahill
'The Gecko', by Leon Gellert
Noli me tangere, by José Rizal

Magpie
'the shadow's keep', by John Anderson
'Nightmare', by Willy Cooper-Kalliguru (trans. C. G. Brandenstein & A. P. Thomas)
'The Magpies', by Dennis Glover
'Magpies', by Judith Wright

Stray Cat
Thomas the Obscure, by Maurice Blanchot (trans. Robert Lamberton)
'Three Sketches of a Favourite Cat', by Sarah Holland-Batt
'Cats of Zamalek', by John Mateer
'Sea Pieces', by John Watson

Eastern Whipbird
'Ab ovo', by Bonny Cassidy
'On Hearing A Whipbird', by Francis Duggan

Pinatubo Volcano
'25' (from *Lyrics II*), '145' (from *Divine Poems*) & '103' (from *Aphorisms III*), by José Garcia Villa
'All about you', 'Outspaced' & 'Giving it over', by Cheryl Pallant

Tarsier
'El Grito' & 'La Soleá', by Federico García Lorca (my trans.)
'Tarsier', by Wislawa Szymborska (trans. Stanislaw Baranczak & Clare Cavanagh)

Satin Bowerbird
'The Satin Bowerbird', by Kate Llewellyn
What is Philosophy?, by Gilles Deleuze and Félix Guattari (trans. Hugh Tomlinson & Graham Burchell)

Moth Orchid
'Moth Orchids', by Ellen Bass
'The Orchid Flower', by Sam Hamill

King Parrot
'Heartbeat', by Roger McDonald
The Waves, by Virginia Woolf

Red-necked Pademelon
'Like a Near Fold' & 'The Floor-Creatures Begin', by Oni Buchanan
'A Man from Benin', by Tomas Tranströmer (trans. Robin Fulton)

Antarctic Beech
'Ancient Woods' & 'Opening Woods', by Peter Larkin
'The Gallery', by Les Murray

Albert's Lyrebird
'And on the Seventh Day', by Oni Buchanan
'A lyrebird', by Michael Farrell
'lyrebird', by Duncan Hose
'Lyrebird', by Les Murray
'Lyrebirds', by Judith Wright

Fallen Myrtle Trunk
'Mountain Myrtle', by Marie E. J. Pitt
'Out of Sorts and Looking at Elms', by Simon West

Housefly
'Up the Country', by Henry Lawson
'Las moscas', by José Emilio Pacheco (my trans.)
'La mosca', by Benito del Pliego (my trans.)

Tea Tree
'O mar e o canavial', by João Cabral de Melo Neto (my trans.)
'Shorelines', by Les Murray
'Lines [Left upon a Seat in a Yew-tree]', by William Wordsworth

Spinifex Termite Mound
'Jus ad bellum, to awe', by Francisco Guevara
Journey to the Stone Country, by Alex Miller
'Contested Landscape at Forsayth', by Les Murray
'At a Lowan's Nest', by John Shaw Neilson
'Termite Lands', by Mark O'Connor
'Song of the Termite Women of Iloata', translated by T. G. H. Strehlow

Hamersley
'Sat. Morning', by Duncan Hose
Altazor, by Vicente Huidobro (Cantos III & V, trans. Eliot Weinberger)
'Driving to Purarrka', 'In the Glow of Early Dawn' & 'Completely Weakened', by Yintilypirna Kaalyamarra (trans. Alexander Brown & Brian Geytenbeek)
'A Stranger to this Country, I'm following them', by Katakapu (trans. Alexander Brown & Brian Geytenbeek)
Spit Temple, by Cecilia Vicuña (trans. Rosa Alcalá)

Lake Mungo
'Lake Mungo', by Susan Fealy
'Scenic Wonders – We Nulla Fellas', by Lionel Fogarty
'Lady Mungo Speaks', by Jeanine Leane

Acknowledgements

Lyre was inspired in part by a writing exercise developed by Jonathan Skinner.

Versions of some of these poems were published in *The Best Australian Poems 2017*, *The Capilano Review* (Canada), *Cordite*, *The Golden Handcuffs Review* (USA), *New Shoots Poetry Anthology*, *Rabbit* and *Verge*. 'Nephology' appeared the chapbook *Departure into Cloud* (Vagabond Press, 2013). 'Stray Cat' was included in the *Animal Intersections* exhibition at the Peanut Gallery, Adelaide, 4–16 July 2017. 'Fallen Myrtle Trunk' was the winner of the 2016 New Shoots Poetry Prize.

The research and composition of this book was generously assisted by a New Work Grant from the Australia Council for the Arts, an Asialink Fellowship to the Philippines, and residential fellowships from Hawthornden International Retreat for Writers, Scotland; Centre d'Art i Natura de Farrera, Spain; Omi International Arts Centre, USA; and Varuna Writers' House. I would also like to thank the School of Humanities, Languages and Social Science and the Centre for Social and Cultural Research at Griffith University for their ongoing support.

Finally, I must thank Pablo, my treasured friend, for his companionship, patience and, at times, frank feedback:

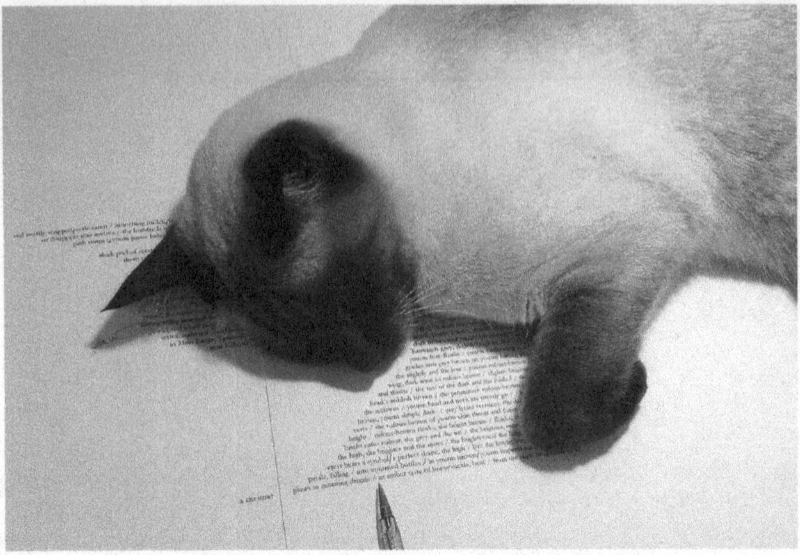

